The

Always

Clean

House

The *Always* *Clean* House

by Rebecca Stafford

Paravelle Publishing
2017

Printed in the United States of America

First Printing, 2017

ISBN-13: 978-0692884324
ISBN-10: 0692884327

Paravelle Publishing
Eugene, Oregon 97405

To the future Mrs. Poulo

Contents

❖ ❖ ❖

The Always Clean House

❖ ❖ ❖

Prepare-Tidy-Clean Room by Room

❖ ❖ ❖

A Little More to Organize

❖ ❖ ❖

Housekeeping

❖ ❖ ❖

Resources

Introduction

An airplane flight crew has a routine to prepare for take off. They do it the same way every time and they have it down to a science. The plane itself is thoughtfully arranged with everything they need and nothing they don't. This preparation makes for a fast turn around and gets the plane in the air on time. No crew member is bumbling around thinking, "I know I've got to get ready for take off but I don't know where to start."

We're going to give our home the airplane treatment with the **Prepare - Tidy - Clean** system.

    Preparing the room creates comfortable flow and function. We will arrange physical surroundings and develop systems to minimize trouble such as bending over or moving things more than once.

    Actual day to day housework is then split into two categories: tidying and cleaning. *Tidying* keeps the house looking nice. *Cleaning* keeps it all sparkly and sanitary.

Clearing Out

"Simplicity is the ultimate sophistication."

- Leonardo DaVinci

An organized and quick-to-clean home begins with choosing what really belongs in it. For most households, this means parting with some of what's already there. Fear not! We aren't tossing everything or throwing out anything that you love - far from it. Rather we're getting rid of some things to allow our favorite things to be seen, enjoyed and more easily maintained. We're just picking out what we want right now - we'll talk about how to put it away and where it belongs later.

Don't give into the temptation to start a few chapters in and skip this crucial first step. The benefits of a good clear out, and indeed the process of clearing out, are many:

- energy & time costs go down: If you don't own it, you aren't spending time or energy cleaning, moving, or repairing it.
- financial cost goes down: A solid clear out makes you think about how many things you buy. Many people find it easier to pass up a purchase once they've seen so many past purchases end up in the donation box.

Even if you aren't paying for offsite storage, ownership is costly. You may end up needing to buy more organizational tools or furnitures, in addition to spending more for services and supplies to clean and maintain these extra possessions.

In the process of the clear out you'll likely find things you thought you'd lost and would need to replace. It's like shopping in your own home.

- enjoyment of your home goes up: Choosing and keeping what you really love increases the percentage of your home that brings you happiness. Beautiful pieces pop out when there is less competing for attention. Pretty dishes, family photos, intricate rugs and travel mementos take center stage when the superfluous is gone. The things you really love and use are not blocked by things that are simply there.

let's get started...

There is no virtue in how many boxes and bags leave the house. There is no correct number of things to own, no correct amount to purge.

> Cull until
> **the majority of what is left brings happiness and function to those who live here**

Gather trash bags, cardboard boxes and a pen & notepad. Hold off on purchasing organizational tools until we know what we've got.

Choose an area - a closet, a shelf, a room. Start culling. For smaller spaces, pull everything out and evaluate it. For large spaces, break the area into smaller sections. For example, don't tackle the entire kitchen. Start with just the pots & pans. Finish each small section before moving onto the next.

The linen closet is a great place to start. The items there are not typically laden with emotion. It's easy to see which bath towels are ready for the rag bin. Before you know it, you've finished an entire closet.

As you pick up an item, sort it into one of 3 piles:
- **keep**
- **trash**
- **let go**

keep
Shift your point of view. It's common to look at an item and ask, 'Can I part with this?' Turn that question around and ask instead, "Is this something I want to keep?"

Cherry pick the things you want, use or need and then toss everything else. Take an underwear drawer. Pull out you favorite panties first. That's your best stuff. Now do a cursory look at the other pairs. Pull out some second choices and everything else can go.

It is only for you to decide what is worth owning. Love shoes? Keep all 200 pairs. Ensure there is enough space, money and time for them by clearing out other things you don't love as much. It's perfectly fine to have more shoes than you need. If they bring you joy, keep them all.

If your grandmother's old mixer is hopelessly broken, but you smile when you see it, keep it. It has become beloved art and belongs in your house.

Keep it because
it makes you *happy* & because you *use* it

trash
Trash is anything broken (except for that mixer) or unsalvageable. Dried up nail polish, old birthday cards, broken earbuds. Trash is

pretty obvious. Gathering up trash is a good assignment for a helper.

let go

Let go of repeats you don't love. If you have two blenders, you probably have one blender too many. The argument "I might need two..." can become "I might need three..." Look over what you have and once again pick out what you want and clear out the rest. If you use the two blenders for two different tasks, keep them both.

When deciding about infrequently used items, see if there is another way you could get the use. For example, if the sewing machine is only pulled out every third halloween, it might be more efficient to borrow or rent a machine than to keep your own on hand.

If you don't use an item, it can probably be let go. If seeing an item makes you feel sad or guilty, toss it.

Where it's going to go? Selling online in your local area is a good option for getting stuff out of the house quickly. You might not get top dollar, but it doesn't take a lot of time and buyers come to you.

Almost anything can be donated to thrift shops and charities. Even cars. There are a few restrictions (some furniture, electronics, etc), so be sure to check their website before loading up anything heavy.

If letting go is tough, try donating to a cause that is special to you. Hospitals, libraries and foster care programs all take relevant donations. There's a place near our house which accepts art supplies and allows the community to use them at their art center. So I donate art and craft supplies there and know it's going to be a lot of fun for someone else. It makes things much easier to part with. This is just one example - consider shelters, schools and rehabilitation programs. Mark each box with where it is going.

As soon as the donation box is full, seal it up and take it away! Load the box right into your car. It's not fun having things rolling around in the trunk, which is great motivation to swing by and make a donation drop. Getting donations out of the house also prevents scavenging and ensures items to go don't end up mingled with keepers.

The "Think-About It" Pile

Some organizers say a maybe pile is a bad idea as it allows you to put off making a decision about an item. I absolutely support a pile of things you still need to think about.

Sorting through the maybes later, you may end up parting with things you didn't think you would at first glance. Remember that these items ended up in the maybe pile in the first place because you acknowledged you might not want or need them anymore.

Just don't let the pile get too large. Try to decide on it right away.

---

as you continue...

Monitor how much physical space you have and keep your possessions pared down to fit.

Keep a donation box at the ready all the time. You're gonna find more to let go as you work. Make collecting it all as painless as possible. Refining your belongings is not a race and it does get easier as you go. This is typically the toughest step toward an always clean home. It's perfectly reasonable to take your time.

With possessions down to just the best stuff, we can start organizing what we've kept.

Organizing

"For every minute spent organizing, an hour is earned."

- Benjamin Franklin

Celebrate your successful clean out! Separating trash from treasure a really tough but crucial step. Now that the foundation is set, it's on to organizing what you've kept.

Organizing is typically a favorite part of the process. It's very satisfying to sort toys into bins, snap on a lid and stack them on the shelf.

There are a lot of tools to keep all of your things orderly and tidy. Elaborate organization systems aren't necessary. For simple and effective solutions, turn to these options:

- **labels**

  Wonderfully useful and very inexpensive, labels are the best way to keep things where they belong. You may quote me on that. Labels are able to communicate in a way that other organizational tools can't. Because they have words.

  Sheets of labels can be run through the printer to produce a neat and uniform finished product. If using the printer is too much, use the same sheets of labels, a pen and good penmanship to make labels by hand. Or write the label out on paper and affix it with a wide strip of clear packing tape to protect it from grime and splashes. For enthusiastic labelers, get a real label maker. There are all sorts

For prominent and attractive labeling, consider metal or wooden label frames. The frame can be screwed directly into a shelf or cupboard door. Paper labels are inserted into the metal frame for a very polished look. Add color or fancy paper to make the labels part of your decor.

- **bins**

In this book the terms 'basket,' 'bin,' 'box' and 'tub' will be used synonymously, as which to use is only a matter of preference and purpose.

Containers with lids are best when bins will be stacked, when storing less frequently accessed items, or to keep the contents out of sight. Lids also keep everything safe from dust and water.

Skip lids if you're trying to encourage access or to work with decor.

Label all bins, even clear ones.

- **hooks**

Clear space by taking what would otherwise end up on the floor and hang from the wall. Easy to see, easy to install.

Things hanging on the wall still have a width (think puffy coats), so be sure that you can comfortably walk by what ever is hanging without the need to turn sideways. (Label hooks, too!)

- **drawer dividers**

Opening drawers shuffles the contents and everything mixes together. It's worth the cost of drawer dividers to keep drawers tidy and useful.

- **shelf dividers**

There are two kinds of shelf dividers. Firstly, there is the type you put over a stack of items (such as dishes) to gain an additional surface for an additional stack of items.

The second kind of shelf divider functions like bookends. They are used to keep unstable piles (such as towels) from merging and eventually bombing whomever opens the cupboard. Divider and conquer.

- **shelf risers**

Take advantage of the vertical storage potential within each shelf by essentially lifting the back of the shelf so that items back there can be seen more easily.

The classic use of shelf risers is in the pantry. Rows of cans and boxes get lost in the back of a deep cupboard. Put the back rows on risers. The risers take up the same amount of space on the shelf, but now we can see and reach everything back there because the back rows they are above the first row of items.

- **creativity**

Experiment with furniture, hooks, shelves, bins, bags, bookcases and dressers. Everyone says, "spice rack" or 'shelf of spices.' But it's perfectly acceptable to store spices in a drawer. I've even seen spice jars stored in an over-the-door shoe organizer. A favorite teacup holds paperclips just as well as a plastic bin will and uses something you *love* to organize something you *use*.

- **the internet**

A mountain of storage inspiration can be found on the internet, giving you a lot of ideas and suggestions for what might work for your family.

let's get started...

Pick a room or space that would make a noticeable difference to have purged and organized. It makes a fun and rewarding project. As with culling, split big jobs into multiple smaller jobs. Organizing will reveal more things that need to be tossed or let go, so keep a trash bag and donation box nearby.

Pull everything out and loosely sort it into categories. Put like with like, even if you don't know where everything is going to go yet. Find a sock with the office supplies? Don't get distracted and start cleaning out the sock drawer. Put the sock in the owner's room and get back to the office supplies.

Now decide which piles need to be subcategorized. For instance, say you're sorting manicure supplies. A big plastic container with a lid to hold it all would be fine. Put in nail polish, emory boards and nail clippers. Label it 'manicure supplies' and put it on the shelf. Done.

But there is also the option to subcategorize. Keep nail files together (in a plastic zip-locking bag or with a rubber band). Put nail polish in smaller bin that fits into the large one, etc. This extra sorting allows you to get to exactly what you're looking for without dumping out a large box of closely related items. How often you access the items and under what circumstances will determines if it would be helpful to subcategorize.

Ziplock bags are perfect for this - they're inexpensive, easily fit into larger containers and do a fine job. Other small or soft sided containers fit well into a larger bin holding the entire category.

How much we own fluctuates; plan for this by leaving a little extra room to expand.

"Make do" with free organizational systems until you're sure it works. For example, use not-quite-right containers you already own until you work out the kinks and know exactly what you need. Or use a nail in place of a hook for a while before investing in fancier options (yes, hooks are 'fancy').

I put up a few nails in the bike shed and told the family to hang bike helmets there rather than on the coat rack where the helmets had been living. I wasn't at all sure they would do it or that it was even the best place for the helmets. But everyone in the family went for it, even asking me to put up real hooks. I'd gotten the family's buy in before I paid for the hooks.

Now you can run out and get some organizational supplies.

where to put it all...
When looking for a place for your stuff, it's tempting to put things where they fit best or where they look nicest. That doesn't always work. There are two mantras for where things belong:

> # It belongs
> ## where you are going to *look* for it

Put it in the most intuitive spot *for you*. If you always look for your hammer in your tool belt, the hammer doesn't belong on your work bench - it goes in the tool belt. Perhaps most people store rubber bands by the paper clips in their desk. But I always look for mine in the kitchen drawer by the twist ties. So that's where the rubber bands continue to live at my house.

> # It belongs
> ## where you are going to *use* it

If highlighters are only used at the desk, keep them near your desk, not with the stationary in your bedroom.

Torn between where you look for it and where you use it, put it where you will look for it. We're making your home intuitive and perfect for you.

Prepare - Tidy - Clean

"Dad took moving pictures of us children washing dishes, so that he could figure out how we could reduce our motions and thus hurry through the task."

- Cheaper by the Dozen

As we've discussed, minimizing daily housework is less about cleaning schedules and vowing to load the dishwasher before going to bed and more about *eliminating wasted motions*. To do this, we use the Prepare - Tidy - Clean system.

prepare

The goal when preparing a room it to create a 1) comfortable, 2) useful, 3) easily maintained space.

Begin by evaluating the purpose or intentions for the space. Be as precise and honest as possible. What do you want to get out of this area?

Let's use a craft room as an illustration. Here you might want a place to set up the sewing machine, a flat surface for making greeting cards and easy access to tidy skeins of yarn. Be specific in your needs. If you would never use a sewing machine for fear of blood loss, don't create a space for the machine to go. It's not part of your custom craft room. Even if it looks nice in someone else's home.

Focus more on what you want than what you think is realistic. Dreaming big is how we stretch possibility. You might just find the extra space you need when you get really excited about what you want.

Survey the room from three heights. First, walk into the room at regular height, not as yourself but as a newcomer. Upon entering the room, where is your eye drawn first? This is the most important place in the room visually. The first view of the room sets the tone for the space. Arrange the furniture and pictures so that these initial focal points are orderly and beautiful.

Now, stand on a chair, balance willing. Look for dusty high shelves and extra storage space that is only visible from atop a chair. Check for awkward corners. With a bird's eye view, you can spot places that will eventually present a cleaning annoyance or storage opportunity.

Finally, hit the floor. There could be great storage opportunities down here as well. Perhaps the bed is surprisingly high, something unnoticed when standing at full height.

Create smooth flow and access to important areas. It is literally a waste of steps to walk around an armchair again and again. Scoot the chair a little. Often moving something just a couple inches makes all the difference. Experiment with different angles and locations for furniture to create natural pathways. Moving furniture for the more useful layout is an ongoing process. We will go into the specifics of preparing each room in upcoming chapters.

To find the best home for your possessions, investigate how often each item gets used. Items used on a daily to weekly basis need to be the most accessible. These things belong in the front of the shelves, in the top drawers and in the most convenient cabinets. These are **primary items**. These are most often used pots and pans, favorite clothes, shampoo, broom - those sorts of things. Observe the family and notice what they use the most often. If something hasn't been used in a month, re-evaluate whether it is unnecessary or is just in the wrong place. A step stool stored in the garage may get no use at all, whereas the very same stool in a bathroom can be a primary item.

Hobbies get primary status. This is very important. If you knit every day, don't squirrel away the project deep in the closet. Keep it out where you work on it. Find a nice basket, fill it with the project's supplies and keep it right out in the open. Home bakers give their standing mixer top billing - right there on the countertop. For many families it is pointless to keep the mixer on the counter, as it is infrequently used and keeping it accessible is taking up valuable counter

---

"Have I shown you my lighter collection?" When I was in high school, I took a trip to visit my aunt which turned into a road trip to see distant relatives I'd never met. Sitting in their living room with my siblings, the old man leaned over and whispered, "Have I shown you my lighter collection?"

He took me and my little brother into a room completely walled with shelves and filled with cigarette lighters. It was the most amazing room I had ever seen. Every lighter was on display and could be picked up and enjoyed. A lighter shaped like a car, the flame coming out of the exhaust pipe. With a boyish snicker, he showed us a naked lady lighter - push one breast and fire shoots out the other.

What stood out to me as much as the lighters was how clear it was that the old man loved them. That is a collection.

---

space.

A teacup collection may not even be physically used at all, but it has value when it brings happiness to those who see it. From that point of view, the teacups are used every single day. Keep treasures out in the open where everyone can enjoy them. It is both sad and awkward to follow a hostess into a back office so she may show off something that makes her happy. Those items are primary, be proud of them and keep them out where they can be seen. A collection undisplayed and under-enjoyed is just storage.

Next we have **secondary items**. These are less frequently used belongings - fancy platters and dishes, cookbooks and guest bedding - that do still get regular use. Supplies for you monthly facial should be accessible but do not need to be on the bathroom counter.

Our final category is **seasonally-used items**. The turkey roaster only used during the holidays, the camping gear and the sand toys that only come out in the summer. These items can be stored in the back of closets and cabinets, in the attic, in the basement.

While they are infrequently used, it is imperative that these seasonal items be properly stored so that they don't end up smashed at the bottom of a big pile.

tidy

Now that the space is arranged for success, we break day to day housekeeping into two categories: *tidying* and *cleaning*. In tidying, we make the room look nice superficially; while cleaning gets rid of the germs and grit in an already tidied room.

There is an episode of the Brady Bunch in which Alice the housekeeper gets replaced by a hardened maid who does the white glove test in the children's bedrooms. My little friend, who lived in a very messy home, was watching it with me and said, "my room wouldn't pass that test!" Then and there I realized cleaning was not the first step of housekeeping. Her room needed a good tidy before dust could even be addressed.

Mentally splitting tidying and cleaning makes sense in a lot of situations. Tidying first and cleaning second prevents the need to carry around cleaning supplies and tools from room to room whether you need to clean there or not. Two separate work sessions is also helpful for those lacking enthusiasm. I tidy and clean back to back, but that is certainly not the only way to do it. Many people prefer to tidy at night and clean in the morning or to tidy before work and clean after dinner. Try it a few different ways and find out what works best for the household.

During a tidy, we pick up all those left behind objects - socks, homework, dirty dishes. We toss crumpled tissues, make beds, load the dishwasher and brush crumbs off of the countertops. Put the shampoo bottle back on the shelf and straighten the chairs.

After tidying, a passive glance sees a neat and orderly room. A closer look would reveal an unswept floor or toothpaste stuck to the side of the sink. This room is not clean, it is simply tidy. The entire house, without a broom or chemical at all, is quickly presentable. Someone dropping by would see an orderly house. And typically the family doesn't mind if the bathroom mirror isn't spotless.

Tidying makes such a difference because it remedies the main messes of life. Our homes don't require daily disinfecting - we're not cutting up raw chicken in the living room. But we are dropping coats, pulling out toys and leaving books around the house. Tidying puts everything back from whence it came and restores basic order.

If you can get everyone in the household to pick up after themselves, even just a little, you've cut out quite a bit of work. With a good clear out and preparation of the room, it will be much easier for everyone to put away their own things. Hopefully they will.

clean

This is when we bust out the cleaners and tools. Cleaning includes washing, vacuuming, dusting and scrubbing. Cleaning is essentially any task requiring cleaners or tools.

The need to clean is less frequent than the need to tidy. Here is where I diverge from traditional advice and say throw cleaning schedules out the window. Floors don't need to be scrubbed every Tuesday. They need to be scrubbed when they're grimy. That may be twice this week and not at all next week. Rather than assigning weekly or monthly time slots for tasks, we can do most cleaning as the need presents itself. In general, don't bother cleaning something that isn't dirty. Check on the work, but don't do it unless you have to.

There are two exceptions to the 'clean as necessary' rule: laundry and the bathroom. We will go into those details in upcoming chapters.

There it is - tidy and clean. Take a last look around the room, checking for missed details. Open the curtains, straighten the rug, fluff the pillows. This extra look takes just a moment and makes the room tight and beautiful. Appreciate your smart work.

Prompts & Checklists

There are two tools for remembering what needs to be done around the house: prompts & checklists

A *prompt* is a simple list of tasks. For repetitive, day to day jobs, prompts work much better than schedule-based lists do.

When should the work be done? Daily? Weekly? There is no need to create a schedule at all. Just run down the prompt and ask yourself, "Does this need to be done today?" If so, do it. If not, skip it.

Prompts clear up all confusion and questions of scheduled cleaning. If the job didn't need to be done today, does it get checked off? Should the job (like dusting) be done anyway, regardless? Should it be rescheduled? Nope. Just move on to the next task.

Do be sure to check the prompt every time. It's easy to get in the habit of skipping vacuuming the stairs because it so infrequently needs to be done. So always check.

A *checklist* is a list of tasks that need to be done once and then checked off. Checklists are handy for the times when a project is large enough that it will take days to complete, making it necessary to keep track of what has or has not been done.

Preparing for a trip, for instance. Did you pack the bathing suits or did your daughter handle that? Did you hold the mail?

Perhaps it was a while ago and you don't have a memory of doing it or not. Check off the tasks as you complete them. Seasonal cleaning is another perfect time for a checklist.

creating prompts & checklists...
Carry a pencil and paper with you while you do the day's housework. In each room, write down all that would need to be done in there to make it perfectly clean. Include vacuuming, dusting and other jobs that are done in every room. Don't go into a ton of detail - just a quick line. Make a list that leaves you confident that if you do everything on the room's prompt, the room will be sparkling.

Laminate your prompt and take it with you from room to room while you tidy and clean. As you're not checking off anything, no need to carry a pencil or print off another prompt tomorrow. Very simple.

Creating a checklist works the same way, except that you include check boxes and plan to use a fresh, blank checklist every time you do the job.

For pre-made prompts and checklists, see the 'resources' section of this book. Personalize the list. If you have no carpet, cross out "vacuum carpets."

Prepare -
Tidy - Clean

Room-by-Room

The Entryway

The entryway is the first - sometimes only - glimpse guests get of your home. It's also where the family is coming in and dropping their things just inside the door.

With all of the coming and going, the greatest plague of the entryway is bottlenecking. An overstuffed and chaotic entry makes it arduous to get anything done and blocks the natural path in and out of the house. The family stacks up by the door, unable to get to their coats and shoes. Throw in the dog and no one is going anywhere quickly.

The entry needs to be 1) useful for entering the house, 2) helpful for leaving it and 3) ready for visitors and guests.

prepare

Stand in the entryway and move around a bit. You should be able to open the front and closet doors without tripping or doing damage. No need to be able to open all of the doors at the same time, of course. There should be enough space to don a coat and (ideally) a place to sit and change shoes.

See to it that everything in the entry has a consistent place to go. Avoid using the entryway floor for any unconfined storage. Even neatly lined up shoes can invite everything to a pile party in the middle of the pathway.

To encourage the hanging of coats rather than the dropping of them, provide a reasonable number of hangers for the size of the closet. Too few hangers and there won't be enough of them for all of the coats; too many and the hangers themselves begin to take up valuable storage space. If your home doesn't have a closet, use hooks attached to the wall or a coat tree (coat trees are great for rentals). Typically storing all outerwear in the owner's bedroom closet doesn't work well. Our bedroom isn't usually our first stop after coming home, so those unhoused coats will likely just end up tossed over a nearby chair.

Do regularly cull coats hanging in the entry. Take out anything that isn't weather appropriate or isn't being used and put them in the closet of the rightful owner.

After school, children often drop their bags at the front door and walk away - at least mine do. Designate a good home for backpacks so they don't stay in this temporary space permanently. Popular storage solutions are the entry closet, hooks, under or in a bench, or in the child's own bedroom (as with coats, getting backpacks directly into bedrooms might be tough, but is doable). Children of any age - certainly those of school age - can be taught to put their backpack where it belongs.

Invest in proper matting. Mats keep out most of the dirt attempting to make its way inside. Most homes have a front porch mat, but don't stop there. Place a doormat on both the inside and the outside of each exterior door. Use mats even in carpeted entryways to save wear and tear on your wall-to-wall carpet. Mats are a low-trouble way to cut down on vacuuming, sweeping and floor damage.

Outdoor mats are the first line of dirt defense and they take a serious beating from the weather. Replace when they become worn or uninviting. Outdoor mats are not meant to be kept forever.

tidy

The entryway is a quick and crucial tidy. Clear up toys, shoes and left-behinds to their proper places. Remind everyone in the family where their stuff actually belongs.

Some items end up in the entry because they are waiting to go somewhere else, such as out to the car or to the neighbor's house. These things mustn't stay in the entryway long enough to get comfortable. Take the library books out to the car to be returned or walk the neighbor's cake pan back across the street.

clean

Cleaning in the entry centers on floors and windows. Sweep the entry daily. Vacuuming may be able to wait a few days between. Muddy foot traffic in the entryway calls for frequent mopping and drying of slick surfaces. Potential water damage is one of the best arguments for keeping things off of the entry area floor. A good snowstorm or water ballon fight reminds us why a cloth handbag might be better placed somewhere else.

If you've glass around or within your door, try to keep it smudge free. These are primary windows that those on both sides of the door will notice. Other windows in the entryway can be cleaned much less frequently.

The Bathroom

Bathrooms are seen as huge cleaning jobs - up there with the kitchen. Unlike in most rooms of the house, everything in the bathroom must be wiped down daily to prevent that build-up unique to bathrooms. It's best to clean up soap scum, stuck-on toothpaste and grime before it becomes visible.

The goal in the bathroom is to 1) prevent gross build up, 2) keep grooming supplies safe and at hand and 3) provide a comfortable bathing space.

prepare

Knowing that we'll be spraying and wiping down the entire room, clear out as many unnecessary or difficult-to-clean objects as possible. The less to move and clean, the more quickly and easily the job will go. Don't overload the bathroom countertops. Instead use the walls for framed artwork and shelves for a limited number of items such as candles.

a bathroom needs...
- **bath mat**
  The ideal bathmat is quick-drying, comfortable to stand on and safe from slippage. A microfiber mat with a rubber or latex

backing fits the bill. Thick cotton mats take forever to dry and should be avoided.

It's common to see a bath towel folded in half and placed on the floor to be used as a bath mat. Even if the used towel was already ready for the wash (thus creating no extra laundry), a towel has all of the downsides of a cotton mat, plus no slip protection.

Before you buy, measure the floor space to ensure you get the right size.

- **shower curtain**

They control a splashy shower, but shower curtains are also magnets for soap scum and bacteria. It's unclear exactly how plastic curtains were ever meant to be cleaned. Instead, the best fabric choice here is polyester. It's impermeable and fast drying. Polyester shower curtains are also machine washable. But you don't need to wash them often. Avoid mildew by completely spreading out the curtain after each shower so the curtain can dry fully.

- **hand towels**

Keep enough hand towels in the linen closet to change the towel in every bathroom, every day. Hand towels get wet and stay wet for a while. Nice and moist for the next visitor. Get thin hand towels to minimize drying time and to save room in the wash and linen closet. Remember that hand towels and bath towels don't have to match.

- **bath towels**

The linen closet needs: # of people in the family multiplied by # of times you plan to change the towels each week. For example, a family of four, washing towels twice a week, needs 8 bath towels. Just eight towels. When I cleaned out my own linen closet, I found I had more than 20 towels cluttering up an already strained cupboard.

Separate out towels that are not used for bathing - beach towels, bath sheets, spa towels. Store these in a more appropriate place, such as on a less convenient shelf. With access to a beach towel, it seems everyone jumps at the opportunity to use way more towel than they need; leaving a full washing machine in their wake. The family will also use what is easiest to get to. Avoid the trouble altogether and store beach towels with the sand toys. Make it easy for the family to do what they are supposed to do.

Install enough hooks or bars for everyone to hang their towel. This prevents towels from landing on the floor or stacking on top of each other on the hook. Label each hook or bar to clear up doubt as to which towel belongs to whom.

- **trash can**

For discretion and to discourage knee-high explorers, use a trash can with a lid. Always line the can with a plastic bag.

tidy

Everyone must put away their own toothbrush and grooming items, hang their own towel and take their things with them when they leave the bathroom. That's not to much to ask, especially with a straightforward bathroom.

Assign and label drawers and personal items such as mouthwash so that everyone feels responsible for their own things and has a place to put their things away.

Ask everyone to take one step back from the sink and mirror when they are combing their hair or brushing their teeth. This keeps hair out of the sink and flecks of toothpaste off of the mirror.

Teach children not to wipe their mouths or faces on the communal hand towel. I've even seen *guests* wipe their mouth on the hand towel.

clean

This is where all the time goes into maintaining a bathroom. Even with good family cooperation, the bathroom is a daily clean.

let's get started...

Daily bathroom cleaning is done using the same cloth for the entire room, working from cleanest surface to grossest.

Presuming the bathroom counters are already tidy, begin with glass cleaner. Spray cleaner directly on your rag and wipe down the "shiny" things - glass, mirrors and fixtures. Spraying your cloth rather than the surfaces prevents overspray onto toothbrushes and such. It also prevents cleaner from getting into the frame of the mirror and causing discoloration and damage.

Once chrome and glass is done, rinse and wring out the rag well. Using the same cloth and all-purpose cleaner, scrub sinks and countertops. There isn't much need for abrasives in the bathroom, as cleaning is done before stubborn messes set in. Rinse the rag as you go. If you do find some sticky messes that just aren't wiping clean, use a little baking soda and it will come right off.

Around the faucet, use a toothbrush. Yes, I'm advocating a 'quick clean' with a toothbrush. But truthfully, the bristle treatment is so much easier and more effective than trying to get scrub those awkward places with a rag. Scrub with the toothbrush and then wipe down with your cleaning rag.

Spot clean cabinets. Wipe down the rim of the tub and any spots off of the walls or shower doors.

Using the rinsed out rag, wipe down outside of the toilet, from the top of the tank to the floor. It sounds like more trouble than it really is.

The outside of the toilet is more important to clean than is the inside. Use a toilet brush to scrub the toilet bowl. Wipe down the rim under the lid with the same rag. Now our rag is used up and we're done.

It seems excessive to do this everyday (if you can't get to it that often, do it every other day) but wiping off a nearly invisible layer of germs is much less repulsive than waiting for yuck to announce itself in force.

Replenish supplies such as soap and shampoo. Try to find a visible or intuitive place for extra toilet paper.

Lastly shake out bath mats and sweep the floor.

Wash out the bathtub and shower pan floor as necessary. Use liquid general purpose cleaner or just baking soda and water. Anything more harsh than baking soda will scratch the surface. Those gouges get lousy with dirt and scum, making them increasingly difficult to clean.

Between scrubbings, simply sweep or hand vacuum out the tub. Dried hair has nothing to stick to when the tub is properly maintained. It just sucks right now.

Wash bathroom floors frequently. We all know what they are exposed to. We aren't eating off of the floor, but we are walking on it. Those same feet prop up on the coffee table. Gross. If you're short on time or interest, *at least* get around the base of the toilet. Usually it's quickest to wash the floor by hand with a rag rather than with a mop. But use a mop if that works best.

Most days cleaning the bathroom is just four steps:
1) wipe down shiny things, 2) wipe down dirty surfaces, 3) scrub the toilet and 4) sweep.
Minutes a day to have an ever-clean bathroom.

The Living Room

This is the first place everyone goes to relax, visit, watch television or just be. For simplicity, I'm going to call this type of room the 'living room' but it applies to any communal area. The family spends most of its time here and we *want* them to spend time out in these common spaces. A tidy room calls out to those looking for a place to relax and makes the room more fun to use.

We want this room to be 1) the quickest tidy in the house, 2) ready for action and 3) comfortable, comfortable, comfortable.

prepare

We need at least some surface space in the living room. To keep the main floorspace clear, opt for small end tables. They fit into awkward or tight spaces and are easier to keep out of the main path.

If the living room is just too small for a table, there are lots of other options. Try a stable tray. A tray can be placed directly on a couch, an upholstered ottoman, or the hearth. And the tray can be put away when it's not in use. It can even be stored under the couch, right at hand. Another awesome choice is a high rail shelf on the wall. When the door bell rings, you can put your book or coffee cup "up high." The cup is out of reach, won't be easily knocked over and there is no extra furniture on the ground. Of course, keep that shelf clear of knick knacks so it can be used as surface space. Think of it as a 'shelf table.'

Have adequate and appropriate lighting for everything done here. There are two types of lighting: general lighting and task lighting.

Typically coming in the form of an overhead fixture, general lighting is the light you get with a flip the main light switch. This light illuminates the entire room. General lighting is an important consideration as it sets the tone of the room. My daughter uses bright, cool white bulbs in her bedroom. To me it feel likes a garage, but she likes it.

Task lighting is just what it sounds like - lighting meant for specific tasks, such as reading, computer use, dining or working on hobbies. Check that the light is bright enough but not glaring. Lamp shades focus light downward, making them great task lighting. Lamps that aim light upward, at the ceiling can be used for general lighting and in dark corners. The better the lighting the more appealing the room is to wanderers-by looking for a place to make camp.

Cut down on fingerprints and trouble by keeping glass in the living room to a minimum. Glass top tables and low hanging mirrors are a nightmare here. Entertainment centers with glass doors are another thing to avoid. If you have low glass, consider covering it with a frosted glass decal. These decals are basically large stickers meant to add decoration or privacy to glass. They camouflage fingerprints and snot smears well.

Blankets in the living room are a nice addition in cool climates. Keep one or two within reach for cuddling up or covering a napping baby. Get a blanket large enough to cover a body comfortably, but not as big as an actual bed. Chenille is good, as is fleece.

Carefully consider whether it is a good idea to allow food in the living room. It is certainly more convenient to allow food. But spills and stickiness are so much more trouble here than they are in the dining room and kitchen. As always, whichever you decide, let the whole family know what the rules are.

tidy

Have a way for each thing *regularly* done in the living room to be contained. A basket for blankets, a dedicated place for remote controls, a box for sheet music. Now tidying is more like sorting. Toss everything back into its bin and...done.

Once things that belong in the living room are restored to their place, clear out what doesn't belong - dishes, clothes, toys, trash, etc. Fold blankets, fluff pillows and open curtains or blinds.

It's up to you to decide what is tidy (or clean) enough for your home. I myself don't really care if the children's toys are out when visitors drop by or while I'm trying to relax in the living room. Toys are ok with me, but it might be different for you.

I concede that tidying a common living space is not a once-a-day task. Some days a tidy will take less than a minute. It really will. Other days "a quick tidy" will seem impossible. That's ok, just skip right over it on your prompt. Persevere.

clean

In all rooms, dust first. Start with one corner of the ceiling and work around the room. Dust inside and out of light fixtures.

Next, wipe down tables and other prime dirty areas with general cleaner and a clean rag. Wipe down windowsills, shelves, fireplace mantles, doorknobs and light switches as necessary. It likely won't be an everyday job. Clean windows and mirrors with glass cleaner and a soft cloth.

In the living room, the floor is used for extra seating space and for playing. Be sure to keep the floors comfortable, too.

Now, vacuum couches and stuffed chairs with the hand vac. Crumbs and, is that sand?, build up under and around cushions. Plan to vacuum couches and carpets at least every few days if food is allowed there.

The Kitchen

To ensure adequate space, modern kitchens have increased cabinets and square footage. I've seen many kitchens, large and small, new and old, and have found no correlation between amount of space and *effectiveness* of a kitchen. It is completely possible to have a small kitchen and amazing function.

Most constructive is to carefully *consider where everything will go and focus on creating work areas*. Though initially tedious, good organization is the most effective way to tip the kitchen scale in your favor.

prepare

The goal is to *cut down on the number of steps* we take in the course of housekeeping. Always be looking for a way to do that.

Assess your space with this in mind. What is your largest asset? The biggest liability? Check out cabinets, floor space, work surfaces. Look for untraditional spaces, such as blank walls which could accommodate shelves. Get up on a step stool and look for more storage. Scrunch down and do the same.

Tailor the kitchen to what you do there the most - cooking, baking, washing up, storing food, eating, entertaining, laundry, etc.

setting up work stations...

Set up stations for the main activities of your kitchen to eliminate some of those wasted motions. Take into account how many things you will need to do and fit into that space. How these stations work depends on the layout and use of your kitchen. Rarely is a kitchen floor plan perfect, so be flexible.

Exactly what goes in each station is unique to your situation, but below is a good basic map.

- **the cooking area**
  Comprises stove, microwave, toaster with access to pots, pans, oil, spices and cooking utensils. Try to be able to reach everything you need for cooking with the fewest steps possible.
- **the baking area**
  Provides easy access to flour, sugar, baking ingredients, the standing mixer and the oven. Keep stirring spoons nearby, too. With the refrigerator between the cooking area and the baking area, you can prepare almost anything without taking more than a half dozen steps. Naturally, if you're not a frequent baker, set up a secondary space for baking and set up a different station in its place.
- **cleaning area**
  Of course the sink, with sponges, hand towels and soap within reach. It's not more fun to clean when you have to cross the kitchen to get a hand towel. Keep the sink empty so that it's always ready for action.
- **preparation/serving area**
  Near dishes, napkins, flatware & serving dishes.

Factor into your layout a plan for keeping work surfaces ready to work. Canisters, toasters, coffee makers and other daily used items can stay on the counters, as long as there is still room for work. Don't store anything on the counter that could suffer from getting wet, such as cookbooks, linens or boxes of food. If you store things on the windowsill, be sure you can still open curtains and windows.

When storing the kitchen trashcan under the counter, get the largest one that you can for the space. Dark spaces like this inspire people to throw garbage blindly. Make the target large. Painting the area a light color makes it a little brighter.

Now that everything has a place... is there any *extra* space? If you've been blessed with the aforementioned large and well-cabineted kitchen, use it to your advantage. Don't get more kitchen items just because you have space for them. Instead, use the vacancy to relieve the pressure on other areas of the house. Begin with items most closely associated with the kitchen - dining linens, a picnic basket, the wet bar.

Label, label, label. This includes in the refrigerator and even where specific items, such as the salad spinner or rice cooker, belong. It actually does help.

there are a lot of ways to save space in a crunch...
- get nesting mixing bowls so that many bowls take up the same foot print as one
- get rid of original packaging. Toss boxes and plastic packaging to save space on shelves. When the potato chips get low, cut the excess bag at the top. This makes it easier to get the remaining chips and it takes up less space.
- hang pots on a rack attached to the ceiling or a wall. I've heard the criticism that hanging pots and pans can collect dust and grease from being out in the kitchen elements. This is completely avoided by only hanging primary pots and pans that will be used often enough to stay clean.
- store cooking utensils (such as wooden spoons and spatulas) in a sturdy jar, vase or crock on the counter. This clears up drawer

space by using counter space. Check that the container won't tip when loaded up and that it won't be in the way.

- don't let cookbooks take over. If you don't have room for them, make room or cull. Copy and store recipes you like, if the cookbook on a whole is not worth keeping. Keep cookbooks in the pantry or library if you've not enough room in the kitchen.
- look for things that can be hung, such as measuring cups. Even a container can be affixed to the wall. So if you can't find drawer or counter space, consider moving on to wall storage.
- use a magnetic strip mounted to the wall to hold knives if a knife block is too much for the counter.
- add shelves to reduce the need for cabinets. The look becomes it own piece of art.

tidy

Tidy the kitchen as you go. Clear countertops, putting away all food stuffs and appliances. Trash makes it into the garbage, bottles go back on shelves.

Load the dishwasher throughout the day, not all at once after a meal. While it is fewer steps to only open the dishwasher once and load it once, it's actually many more steps to work around a pile of precariously stacked dirty dishes or full sink all day.

A schedule for when and how often to run the dishwasher will naturally present itself. It may work out that best to run the dishwasher after lunch and have it unloaded when dinner preparation starts. Perhaps it is best to run it overnight or while you're at work. Use whatever schedule means clean dishes when you need them and adequate time to load and unload.

Typically we scrub and sweep during the cleaning stage. In the kitchen, however, tidiness requires that there are no crumbs on the counter. Wipe the countertops clean. Sweep the floor.

All tidy yet the kitchen still looks a little messy? Reassess what you are storing where and see if you can't remedy whatever is causing the eye clutter.

clean

The kitchen work surfaces must be sanitary at all times. Bleach and antibacterial soap are not necessary, but remember that food is being prepared here. We do not want cross contamination or to prepare food on dirty surfaces. Suspect counters make for a suspect kitchen.

Grease and food splatters get everywhere! Spot clean walls, cabinets and appliances each day. Don't worry about getting every single smear or wiping things completely down. Just try to keep up with day to day spots.

Plan to clean out the fridge once a week. Do it the day before garbage day or the day before grocery shopping day.

On the topic of refrigerators, invest in good food storage ware. Glass storage containers are best, as they don't retain stains or flavors. Put all the lids in a narrow bin and stack the containers. It makes putting away food a breeze. It also maximizes the fridge 'shelf life' of food by ensuring it's properly sealed and preserved.

The Dining Room

The dining room is one of the home's central multi-purpose rooms - used daily for nearly everything. Paying bills, eating, art projects, entertaining - it all happens here.

prepare

It's easy for the dining table to be overtaken by paper and projects. It begins innocently enough. Let's just scoot this project to the other end of the table while we eat dinner. Large tables are often able to hold both a meal and a stack of papers. And once in a while, it's harmless enough. But little messes don't stay little for long. And even a small stack of paper can interfere with the other things done at the table. So have a short term plan for where those unfinished projects will go when dinner time comes. For example, in our home short term projects - homework or artistic ventures - get placed on my nearby desk, as it's reliably clear and very convenient to the dining room.

Skip the traditional rug under the dining table. Even adults knock over a glass now and then. A rug multiplies the work of such a clean up by ten. They are so pretty though...

Tablecloths protect the table from scratches, food and drink. If you don't use tablecloths regularly still have at least one tablecloth on hand for each season.

Get the nicest tablecloths for occasions when your table will be accommodating a leaf. We most often put the table leaves in when entertaining a large group - exactly when we want to have nice linens. Less fancy tablecloths are fine for everyday use.

Sometimes a tablecloth just doesn't make sense. Babies and toddlers leave a lot of spills and food smears - messes most easily cleaned with a sponge, not a washing machine. For very nice tables, however, use a tablecloth to protect the finish.

Space available, it's particularly convenient to store table linens in the dining room as this is where they will be used. Create useful space in a large dining room by bringing in a pretty bureau or side table. A bookcase featuring bins or baskets also provides discreet linen storage.

tidy

Tidy up and straighten chairs throughout the day. It's a little thing but really makes the dining room look sharp. Despite its extensive use, the dining room is a quick tidy. That's because these items are temporary and haven't gotten comfortable. If someone has walked away from a large project, drag the offender back into the dining room and have them pick it up.

clean

Cleanliness in the dining room is *critical*. Food is served and eaten here so it must be hygienic. This is also where you might lay out business and homework so the table can't be sticky or wet.

From time to time, wipe down the chairs. Focus mostly on the top of the chair back, where one grabs the chair to pull it out from the table. At least seasonally, wipe down the table legs and the chairs - they get dirty and sticky, too.

How often to mop depends on how clean the eaters in the home are. If there is only one messy eater, save time by only washing under his or her chair.

The Bedroom

W ake up one morning and just lay there. What would make this a perfect room to wake up in? What about an easier room to use? You have my permission to stay in bed as long as it takes to make a plan.

prepare

stock the bedroom with the must haves...

- **two full set of linens**

  A set of linens consists of a fitted (bottom) sheet, a flat (top) sheet and a pillowcase for each pillow.

  It is often mistakenly recommended to have *three* sets of linens - one on the bed, one folded in the closet and one in the laundry pile waiting to be washed. Entirely ridiculous. Laundry doesn't sit in the hamper long enough to warrant three sets. Babies and those who wet the bed may require an extra set but two sets is sufficient for most beds. Save the space.

  Find the right balance between softness, durability and ease of care. The higher the thread count, the less durable the fabric. While creating my bridal registry, I ran into something I'd never seen before: one thousand thread-count sheets! I added the sheets to my wishlist and did, in fact, receive them. They were so creamy soft; nothing like the ropey sheets of my childhood bunk bed.

The esteemed sheets lasted about five months, full of large holes by the end. See, in order to fit 1000 threads in a square inch, the threads must be extremely thin and those thin threads are more likely to break. (For reference, the indestructible sheets of youth are 200- or 300- thread count.)

Always use a mattress pad under the bedsheets to protect the mattress and aid in cleaning, even for sleepers who can hold their liquids. These are not "plastic sheets." They feel and sound just like regular fabric, but are waterproof. They are also machine washable. It's far cheaper to replace a mattress pad than to replace an entire mattress. Protect pillows with a zipping case or use two pillowcases, facing opposite directions. A dust ruffle does a great job hiding under the bed storage. A regular fitted sheet on the box spring is a stylish alternative to a dust ruffle if you have nothing to hide.

- **a primary blanket**
  A duvet, quilt or comforter. This will be your main blanket.
- **a thinner blanket or two**
  For layering on cold nights. Thin blankets can be added on top or made right into the bed for convenience. Thinner blankets are easier to launder than are thick comforters.
- **a flashlight**
  Keep a flashlight near the bed. It comes in handy for midnight power outages and when investigating scary monster noises.

What do you do before bed? Many sleepers start with some hand cream or reading. Have a table, drawer, shelf or basket near the bed to contain these items and save yourself a trip out of the warm bed to grab a book.

As you arrange furniture, be sure to leave a clear path to the main door and to the bathroom. The middle of the night is a terrible time to realize there's been a decor malfunction.

tidy

Once the kinks are worked out, bedrooms take less than 4 minutes to tidy in the morning; most of that spent making the bed.

Straighten everything - rugs, night stands, dresser tops, curtains. Put laundry in the basket. Shut the closet door.

Make the bed...or don't. If you're not one to jump out of bed and start making it first thing in the morning, fear not. Beds benefit from a good air out before blankets get tucked into place anyway. You can safely attend to bed making later in the day. It's unlikely a guest will stop by to see your bedroom. But always make the bed before dusting.

When you leave, take *everything* that doesn't belong with you.

Is there a little someone sharing your bedroom right now? Keep his or her stuff close at hand but be discerning about what gets to stay in your room. There is no need to have extra empty bottles in the bedroom, for instance. Those are best kept where they will be used - in the kitchen.

Next, contain the baby's mess. An extra dresser drawer is the best option. Close the drawer and all trace of extra sleepers is gone. If a drawer is not an option, use bins. Have a bin for diapers and wipes - the things you need for a midnight diaper change. Have another bin for bedtime books or a change of clothes or anything else you need to keep in the bedroom. Put those bins in a convenient place. Now it's a breeze to tidy up. Just toss baby's things into the proper bins.

clean

Bedroom cleaning is light work. Wipe surfaces down and clean glass and mirrors of fingerprints and smudges. Keep linens fresh and clean at all times. No crumbs, no sweaty pillows. Plan to change and wash bedding about once a week. Comforters don't need to be washed frequently. Instead air out pillows and comforters. The simplest way is to take them outside to enjoy the breeze while the sheets are in the washer.

Children's Bedrooms

Children make much more use of their bedrooms than do adults. They play here, entertain friends here, dream and sleep here. Take the time to prepare a good space for them that is fun, useful and streamlined for keeping clean and tidy.

prepare

Get children involved in preparing and staging their bedroom. Solicit information about how the room is working right now. Ask if shelves are at a good height. Are there enough bins, baskets, tubs and drawers to contain everything? Some of the answers will be intuitive; some may surprise you. Children might not be able to suggest a solution; you're mostly just asking for a list of the problems.

Most toys and clothes in a child's room should be in active use. What does that mean? That everything in the room is enjoyed. Outgrown clothes and broken toys block the function of the room and overwhelm children. As you clear and organize, question whether each thing is being used.

Ensure there is plenty of room to put away clothing. If drawers and closets are overflowing, it's no wonder clean laundry ends up on the floors. Go through each child's clothing seasonally. Check that everything fits and is still being worn.

Store "grow-into" clothes not in dresser drawers but in a separate, labelled container.

Original packaging is rarely useful for storage and is usually meant to be disposable. Throw away the crushed cardboard boxes and find good permanent containers. And...label.

Don't stack containers too high on shelves; three high at the most. Children are prone to yanking out whichever bin they're after and the entire precarious tower collapses.

Toys can come into the bed but they must still all have another spot to be put away. Sleep is important, don't wreck it by *storing* 40 stuffed animals on the bed. Come up with an accessible place for children to find and enjoy lovies without a bed filled with them.

Make pulling books out of the bookcase effortless. It's a subtle way to encourage reading and literacy. If children can't find or easily access books, they might stop looking for books at all. Ensure that there is wiggle room on the shelf.

A child's room can quickly fill with mementos from their tiny pasts - beloved baby toys, first occasion outfits and delicate gifts. Get them out of there! It is a *huge* burden for a child to care for such special items. Along with the risk of damage to these mementos, tiptoeing around and constantly moving these things makes the room less enjoyable. Get a quality container and tuck away these treasures. Safe and stored all together, they will be wonderful to rediscover and share with the children later. The items will then be exciting, not annoying.

Once you've set up and arranged the room, keep a watchful eye on how the room is working (or not). Children are very honest and their actions will let you know how things are going. Double check that children have the tools and skills to tidy the room to your standards. Repeat problems indicate a need for change. Be flexible and prepared for some fine tuning.

Is the room still just too full? If so, it might require a second purging. But when doing a second purge, don't hit the *floors* with a garbage bag and a donation box. Now this is very important: go after the things that are *not* on the floor. The toys out on the floor right now are the ones the children have been playing with, the toys they clearly want and use. Instead, weed through the toys and clothes they've left untouched.

tidy

Remind young children to pick up their toys every time they're done playing. Easier said than done. Take it as a maxim, not a standard.

Even small children can be charged with putting their own laundry in the hamper and books and toys back where they belong. Praise their effort.

Little children can even be responsible for making their beds with the right preparation. Minimize bedding; one blanket is preferable to layering many blankets, as one is much easier to wrangle. Bottom and top sheets are both still necessary, unless you're willing to wash the blanket frequently. If you're worried about the wear and tear from repeated washings, get an inexpensive comforter and pack away heirloom quilts for a while.

For older and younger children alike, make sure that dirty laundry and garbage always make their way out of the bedroom.

If you find yourself struggling to tidy the room, imagine how the *children* must feel when they face it.

clean

A weekly spray and wipe treatment takes care of most bedroom cleaning. General cleaners are safe for use in the nursery and children's bedrooms. That doesn't mean you can leave a bottle of glass cleaner on the changing table. But the children can taste their dresser without being poisoned.

I encourage parents to do the cleaning in a child's room until the child is about eight years old. Cleaning is more challenging than tidying. Children can (sort of) tell when their toys are on the floor. But the same children are oblivious to sticky finger prints on glass. They honestly don't know when the windowsills need to be wiped down. They simply don't *see* dirt. Add to this using chemicals and being responsible for what happens with them, and it is best to clean a child's bedroom a little longer than you would tidy the room for them.

a few words about working with children...

Hold back. Try not to redo a child's work. Once the responsibility has been delegated to them, respect the job they've done. If the child can't do it, teach him. If he *won't* do it, teach him again. Every time he claims to be incapable of the job, offer to teach him again. Eventually, he'll get tired of being taught again and again and just might comply.

Do your own thorough tidy and clean in the children's rooms every so often. It gives children an occasional clean slate and gives you the opportunity to evaluate the systems and contents of the room.

Always follow up with organizational support. A father once came to me with the complaint that he couldn't even get into his sons' room because the boys never put away their clean laundry. A little prodding on my part revealed his sons didn't have dressers! Where exactly did he expect them to store these clothes? Furthermore, it had been years since he'd sorted through their clothes. His boys were managing wardrobes of all different sizes and seasons. Of course they couldn't handle it! Once the storage and sorting had been worked out, the boys' problem largely went away.

Finally, try to stay calm about messes. Worry is only warranted if the mess has become dangerous or has crowded the child out of his room. I say that in jest, but it does happen. Play migrates to common spaces when the bedroom gets too messy - a good sign it's time to check on the state of Junior's room.

The Laundry Room

Often overlooked, the laundry room is one of the hardest working in the house. To make washing laundry as pleasant as possible, stock the shelves and keep the room clean and organized.

prepare

Stock the laundry shelves with everything necessary to do the laundry and nothing else.

laundry room essentials...

- **laundry detergent**
  One type of laundry detergent is probably enough, though some households use two kinds - one for usual wash and a more delicate detergent for special wash or baby items.
- **dryer sheets/fabric softener**
  You only need one or the other. Take care not to use too much fabric softener. Over time fabric softener builds up and leaves a coating on the fibers. This build up makes items difficult to completely clean and gives clothes a musty smell. Towels especially suffer when they can't dry out properly. To remove this build up, periodically wash laundry with vinegar rather than fabric softener.
- **stain remover**

- **vinegar**

  Vinegar is wonderfully useful. Add vinegar to a load of laundry using the fabric softener compartment of the washer. Vinegar removes fabric softener residue and starch build up. Don't worry, it doesn't leave an odor behind.

- **bleach**

  To whiten fabrics and get rid of mildew

- **borax**

  This naturally occurring mineral salt acts a deodorizer and laundry detergent booster. When bleach is too harsh, use borax in its place. There is a clear difference between a load washed with just detergent and one with detergent and borax. It is safe to use with colored clothing and really makes whites whiter.

- **laundry baskets**

  Have separate baskets for clean laundry coming out of the dryer and for dirty laundry waiting to go into the wash. Dirty laundry makes for a dirty laundry basket. Make sure the baskets can be differentiated by using labels or different colors.

  Keep clothes hampers in children's rooms small and empty them often. Children's clothes are especially small. By the time the laundry pile fills the basket, the child can be nearly out of clothes.

- **iron**

  Ironing with starch causes build up and that means cleaning the iron. Begin with a cool, empty and unplugged iron. Clean the metal face of the iron using a paste of water and baking soda. Baking soda is a gentle abrasive and won't damage the iron. Use a cotton swab to clean the steam holes, taking care not to get baking soda (or anything else) in the holes. Wipe down the exterior, including the entire cord, with a wet cloth.

- **an ironing board or mat**
- **clothesline (optional)**

If you plan to use a clothes line, invest in a good one. Install it in a convenient place and make sure it is well-secured. All of the family's laundry can be line dried, with the exception of fabrics that stretch (such as wool) which should be dried flat, most anything can go on the line. Hanging your laundry on a clothes line is very efficient; the sun was going to be there anyway. In wet climates, consider installing your clothesline indoors.

Add your own labels to cleaning bottles. "Laundry Detergent," "Bleach," etc. With clear and uniform labels, when I tell my daughter to spray a stain with stain remover, she is able to pull the bottle labelled "stain remover" rather than asking me exactly which squirt bottle is the right one.

It's also a life saver when teaching children to do their own laundry. Children can get confused by tons of writing and advertising claims all over the bottles. Label them clearly and avoid the entire issue. Don't take off the original labels, however, as you do want to be able to read the instructions and cautions.

tidy
Put laundry in the proper hamper. Empty trash.

clean
Wipe down all surfaces in the laundry room from time to time. Get the shelves, the exterior of appliances and countertops.

Washing machines can get so dirty that it's a mystery how they get clothes clean. If you notice clothes coming out looking dirtier than they did when they went in, it's time to clean the washer.

There are two good options for doing this. First, using special washing machine cleaner, available at the grocery store. It works very well and I would recommend it. The washer can be cleaned by cleaned running the empty washer with bleach and hot water. Then run it again with white vinegar to rinse it clean.

Flush out washing machine dispensers for detergent, fabric softener and bleach by pouring warm straight vinegar into them. Wipe the outside of both the washer and dryer with a wet rag.

Periodically wipe out laundry baskets.

A Little more to Organize

The Grounds

It's just as easy to keep outdoors tidy as it is the indoors. Keep up on the home's exterior and it's little trouble. Just remember to mow every now and then.

prepare

Let's take a walk across the street and get a good look at your home. Take in the entire picture: the grounds, porches, balconies, plants, pathways, fences, fountains, etc. What is the house and yard saying? Maybe the scooters tucked under the eaves tell passersby that children play happily here. Perhaps the spiderwebs around the porch don't look very welcoming.

A friend of mine who had a toddler once asked a neighbor if she could have the rotting plastic slide that had been discarded in the neighbor's front yard for years. Apparently, that neighbor's yard was saying, "Please help me get rid of my moldy toys!"

Start a list of what needs to be done. Look for left out toys, garbage and out of control foliage. Check the weeds in the cracks of the sidewalk and whether the grass needs to be edged. Oil in the driveway? Need new gravel or wood chips? Don't run off and start - just write it down. Note projects big and small. It won't all get done at once, so it's good to have a comprehensive list.

Back on your own side of the street, clean up all trash and move things that don't belong. The yard should absolutely not be used for random storage. A dismantled bed frame, piles of items on their way to the car and stacks of cardboard boxes are not appropriate outside storage. They are ugly and get damaged in weather. If you're willing to store it in those conditions, you might as well toss it completely.

Trash is gone. Items that didn't belong have been relocated. Now let's get to using the space you've created. All that's left outside are things that belong outside: hoses, outdoor furniture, potted plants, etc.

Using the same principles as when preparing and arranging common spaces, determine where your furniture will go.

Be sure important doors are accessible with your furniture layout. When doors are blocked, the flow in and out is lost. This makes it cumbersome to use the outdoor space and so it's sure not to get as much use as it could. When a possible layout is found, go back inside the house and make sure nothing is blocking the pretty view out the window from indoors.

Perhaps more than anywhere else, things kept outdoors need good containers and covers to protect it from damage. Purchase as many hose holders as there are hoses. If the grill needs a cover, get that, too.

Take periodic walks back across the street.

tidy

Tidying outdoors centers on picking up debris and left-behinds as you see them.

Garbage blows in and gets stuck in the grass and bushes; pick it up as you walk by.

Reset everything on the porch back to its proper place once in a while. Return toys to their proper homes. Arrange outdoor chairs. It literally takes seconds, not even a full minute.

clean

It sounds funny, but there can be a fair amount of cleaning to be done outdoors. It doesn't need to be done often, just well.

Sweep porches, decks and walkways. While you have the broom in hand, sweep away cobwebs from lights, rafters and railings. A stiff whisk broom also works very well for getting down sticky webs.

Wash the doors, especially if you have pets or a lot of mud. Shoe and paw prints need to go. Wash the mailbox, light fixtures, window frames and dingy house numbers.

In the end, the outside is the outside and it is impossible to keep the outdoors spotless.

Take care to prepare the grounds and house exterior for the upcoming season. When the warm weather comes, bring out all you need for a fun summer. As it grows colder outdoors, check your home's weatherproofing, lay in supplies such as firewood, and put away anything that won't be used during the cold months.

The Car

Family vehicles are traveling domiciles with all the same joys and trouble of home. For smooth sailing, be prepared for the most common on-the-go problems.

prepare

It's crucial that everything in the car has a place. Store things in the most intuitive spot in the car. Extra sunglasses get a place with quick driver access. Jumper cables can be stored in the way back.

I used to keep carsickness bags in the car kit. However, with the kit in the *back* of the car and the children vomiting in the *middle* of the car and me driving in the *front* of the car, we had a problem. The bags couldn't be used, though they were frequently needed. So now the bags are stored in the pockets behind the front seats - the pockets directly in front of back seat passengers. When the children feel nauseous, the bags are right there.

Store maps together, along with parking or entrance passes to national forests, et cetera. But don't store it in the car unless there is good reason. In general, keep as little in the car as possible. Just take the package (use a large manilla envelope) along on adventures and you know that you have everything you'll need.

things to consider keeping in the car...

for passengers

- extra clothes for small children, down to socks and underpants.
- small amount of potable water
- small first-aid kit: bandaids, antibacterial ointment, tweezers. Don't go overboard. Bandaids will cover most 'emergencies.'
- small medicine kit: throat lozenges, fever reducer, pain reliever
- a few empty plastic bags for garbage or wet clothes
- thin towel(s) and washcloths
- pre-moistened hand wipes
- hard candy and gum. Both are long-lasting distractions for car sick children
- personal items, such as feminine products and breastfeeding pads
- seasonal items such as mittens or bathing suits

for pets

- extra leash
- plenty of doggy bags
- water bowl. The collapsable type takes up the least amount of room.
- small bag of treats
- ball or toy
- something to gnaw on

for baby

Have a bare bones 'diaper bag' for the car. This cache doesn't take the place of planning and an actual diaper bag, but it fills in the gaps.

- diapers
- wipes
- washcloths
- change of clothes

- empty bottle/sippy cup/binky

for the car
In a completely separate container, gather the tools for trouble
involving the physical car. These tools can be stored in a remote
location of the car, such as the trunk of the car or truck bed
toolbox.
- jumper cables
- strong flashlight with batteries
- tire repair kit of everything required to change a tire.
- basic tool kit, including a tire pressure gauge and duct tape.
- rope
- helpful car manuals. Only keep in the car manuals you would
  actually use on the road.
- For climates with extreme weather, include chains for snow or
  extra water for overheating. Rotate out seasonal equipment as
  it takes up a lot of space.

Once the car contents is ready, get containers that fit comfortably
in your car and will hold everything you plan to store in it.

buckling up...
Color code the seat buckles to its corresponding strap
attachments. A stripe of red on a buckle, a stripe of red on the
strap. The next buckle and strap are labeled in blue, the next
green, etc. Animal stickers are great, too. Now children can get
settled into their seats quickly. No complaining and snatching
each other's buckles.

tidy

Take everything (purchases, cups, trash, etc.) along with you
when leaving the car to go into the house. Teach your little ones
to do the same. This will cut car tidying down significantly.

Do a sweep in the back seat every so often to see that everything is making its way inside.

clean

Clean the car as you would the house - dust, wash and vacuum. Wipe down interior surfaces as they get dusty. Plain soap and water is fine, but for a nice shine use vinyl cleaner and glass cleaner. Vacuum the car interior regularly.

As for the car's exterior, it would seem that washing a car in the driveway would be the most green way to go. It's certainly less expensive. But with the hose & bucket method, all of that soap, dirt, gasoline and oil runs into storm drains and eventually into rivers and streams, contaminating the water and ecosystem. Commercial car washes, on the other hand, must meet standards for water efficiency and disposal of chemicals. These standards make car washes, counterintuitively, a more environmentally sound option.

Between washes, clean mirrors and windows both for safety and class. Always give the car a good tidy and clean before and after a long trip.

The Medicine Cabinet

A safe and useful medicine cabinet hinges on good organization and oversight. If you can't find it, you can't use it. If it's expired, you shouldn't use it.

let's get started...
Open up that medicine cabinet and pull everything out. Collect all of the medicine and medical supplies from around the house. The aspirin from the bathroom, the bandaids from the kitchen drawer - gather it all together and get ready to sort.

As we sort, toss anything expired or suspect or no longer necessary. Most medications can be thrown away in the regular trash can. Don't flush drugs down the toilet unless the label specifically says to. Put expired or unwanted medication into another container, such as a bottle or bag, before throwing it in the trash to prevent pills from falling out of the trash bag.

Make piles according to what ailment or body part the medication treats or what the type of medication it is.

medication groupings...
quick-aid/first-aid
- hydrogen peroxide to clean wounds
- Neosporin or other anti-biotic ointment
- hydrocortisone for skin inflammation from insect bites and skin allergies

- isopropyl alcohol
- bandages of different sizes, including butterfly bandages. Liquid bandages are helpful for awkward places or on hands.
- tweezers for removing glass or splinters
- thermometer. Make sure you know how to use it properly.
- gauze
- medical tape

pain relievers
The most often used medications are simple over-the-counter pain relievers. Keep them accessible and in stock.

- aspirin - pain killer, anti-inflammatory and fever reducer.
- acetaminophen - fever reducer.
- ibuprofen - anti-inflammatory and reduces swelling.
- naproxen - muscle relaxant
- the same medications in child-appropriate forms

prescription medication
In general, prescription medications are powerful and controlled substances. As the medicine cabinet will be used by anyone and everyone in the family, it's advisable to keep doctor prescribed medications away from common access.

other maladies
With everything else separated out, the rest of the medication on the table can be sorted by what symptoms they treat. These are the over-the-counter creams, syrups and pills we use to treat symptoms or pain from specific conditions.

Store each pile, even if there is only one medication in that pile, in zipping plastic bags or another small container. Mark each bag clearly with what affliction or symptom it treats. When a sickie wants to know what's on hand for indigestion, he can pull out one bag and see all of his choices. If a medicine treats two symptoms, just put it in the pile you'd be most likely to turn to. Remember - put it where you're going to look for it.

a few other helpful items to have on hand
- epi-pen for known allergic reactions
- hot/cold packs
- aloe vera for relief from sunburns and skin inflammation
- calamine lotion to treat itchy skin
- cloth bandages

If someone in the family has a chronic condition treated with over the counter medications, let's say seasonal allergies, keep enough of that medication on hand. Otherwise, purchase medication as necessary. This saves both money and space, with a small inconvenience of making a trip to the store when you need some couch syrup.

Add maintenance of the medicine cabinet to your checklist of seasonal cleaning duties. Replenish as supplies run low. A quick culling during seasonal cleaning is all it takes to maintain a tidy, healthy medicine cabinet.

Household Toolbox

It's tempting to put off simple projects. And it doesn't make the job more fun when fixing things involves digging through a deep toolbox in a cold garage. Dodge all the trouble by compiling a primary toolbox to keep in the kitchen or hall closet. Handy makes for useful.

This small tool box is not a complete workshop. Fill it with just the most helpful tools.

tools to consider keeping in your indoor toolbox:
- **hammer**
- **small nails**
  Store nails in a container that 1) fully closes (spilled nails are literally a pain to clean up) and 2) doesn't allow sharp tips to poke through.
- **screwdrivers**
  A flat head and phillips-head. A two-in-one is great.
- **pliers**
- **retractable tape measure**
- **ruler**
  It's handy to have both a ruler and a tape measure
- **sharpened pencil**
- **permanent marker**
- **flashlight with batteries**

extra tools to consider including:

- **pliers**
- **clippers**
  For arranging bouquets or pruning houseplants
- **utility knife**
- **tape**
- **cloth tape measure**
- **adjustable wrench**

Store the tool box in a convenient place to ensure you can use it.

Seasonal Baskets

Swimsuits in the summer, scarves in the winter - each season brings its own accessories to need frequently and lose frequently.

Rather than running from room to room searching for missing swim goggles, keep a bin in an easy access spot to serve as a catch-all for the season's accessories.

compiling your seasonal basket...
In the *warm weather*, fill it with swim goggles, bathing suits, sunglasses, sun hats. In *colder months*, swap out for gloves, warm hats, scarves.

This saves an unbelievable amount of time both when tidying and when getting everyone out the door, which is why I had to include this chapter.

Just be sure that everything is clean and dry before it goes back into the basket. When children are rushing out the door, it's nice to be able to reach into the winter basket and pull out a hat and mittens.

Books & Such

Encourage reading by making it easy to see what you have and get your hands on the right book.

let's get started...
Gather up all your books and separate them into three categories: reference, fiction and non-fiction. As you sort, set aside unwanted books to donate. Sort into one of these categories:

reference
Reference books, like encyclopedias and dictionaries, are often prettier than our other books. Put them on display by keeping these books in a prominent place or where you will see them when you first enter the room.

fiction
Fiction allows the most creative shelving. Consider these options:
- Alphabetically by author's last name. This works well if you can remember the author of the book you're searching for. It also means other books by the same author will be nearby.
- By genre. For example, romance novels, classic literature, junk fiction, book club picks, etc.

- By color or size. This is an artistic pursuit and really fun to do. We're usually familiar enough with our books to pick them out, even without a rigid organizing systems.

non-fiction

Non-fiction books are books on real events or on a general topic.

When organizing non-fiction we want all the books on the same topic together, not necessarily books by the same author together.

Rough sort non-fiction into broad categories. For example, separate them into biographies, nutrition, etc. You can sort into more and more detailed categories - for instance, rather than having just a general foreign language section, refine it even more into Italian, French, German, etc.

Don't shelve non-fiction by color. It is too difficult to gather all of the books you want when researching a single topic.

favorites

Everyone has a subject or two (for example: fishing, Vikings or art history) which make up a good portion of their library. Set aside these books for their own shelf, separate from the other non-fiction books. We want to be able to grab these books easily and the collection, set apart, is its own reminder of what you love.

magazines

Keep two magazine issues back, plus the one you're currently reading. If you need a little more time or you're an extreme magazine reader, allow yourselves four issues. Anything more than that is probably not going to be read.

Put magazines where you read them - the bathroom, by the couch, even in the car if that makes the most sense for your lifestyle.

books from the public library
Designate *one* place to keep books checked out from the public.
Any basket, tote or shelf dedicated will do as long as the books
will be kept together. Books are very heavy; make sure your
carrying method is strong enough for them.

As you come across borrowed library books (because they
will still end up all over the house), return them to the basket or
shelf. When it's time to head back to the library, grab the entire
basket or bag. Return everything to the library and your basket is
ready to be filled up again.

Housekeeping

The quotes in the upcoming chapters are from *Mrs. Elizabeth Beeton's Book of Household Management*. Mrs. Beeton became a wife at a time when the country was shifting from agrarian to city life. Living in the city, she wrote her book after seeing that many women didn't know how to manage a home in this new environment.

Her book gives timeless advice and also provides an eye-opening glimpse of what our foremothers dealt with. They had to chop the wood to heat the water for their wash tub for goodness' sake! Modern conveniences take care of most of our housework for us. Technology runs the vacuum cleaner, washes our dishes and dries our laundry. The reader gets a warm feeling of the relative ease of modern housework.

Enough 'starving people would be happy to have that.' On to housekeeping.

Cleaners & Tools

With the right cleaners and tools, housework doesn't take as long to complete. Having the right tools streamlines the work - always eliminating wasted motions and trouble.

must have tools...
- **cloths/rags**
  Use real cloth rags, not paper towels. Paper towels seem convenient but with a bin of cloth rags in a handy place, cloth is just as convenient. Cloth works better and makes more sense economically and environmentally. If the cloth rag gets particularly gross or oily, you can still toss it in the trash without guilt.

  Cut up an old bath towel or use washcloths that have seen better days. When a washcloth is retired to the rag bin, snip off one corner to identify it as a rag.
- **toilet scrub brush**
  Most households find a toilet brush to be a "must have," although feel free to opt for yellow gloves and a sponge.

  Toilet cleaning systems with disposable heads are also available. They are billed as disinfecting and more hygienic. But how often is someone drinking from the family toilet? Borax or bleach does a fine job. Disposable cleaning items, in general, produce a lot of waste and come soaked in unknown chemicals.

And they really aren't any more useful or convenient than a plain toilet brush.

- **toothbrush**

Useful when cleaning tight places, such as around drains and faucets. With the tough work they do, toothbrushes run out of bristly power and need frequent replacing. Get extras by snatching up used toothbrushes headed for the garbage.

- **sponges**

Have multiple sponges in use at a time - one for the kitchen, one for general housework, one for the bathroom to prevent cross contamination. Clip one corner of the sponge to mark it as a housework sponge and two corners for the bathroom. Leave the kitchen sponge intact.

- **stiff brush with plastic bristles**

To be used for cleaning tiles or particularly grimy floors. Most cleaning won't require such tough measures, but when it does, you'll really need that stiff brush.

- **spray bottles**

Put homemade cleaners or cleaners purchased in bulk into spray bottles. Label the bottles clearly. Don't reuse any bottles which have held chemicals.

- **rubber cleaning gloves**

Sometimes we subconsciously avoid cleaning because we don't want to get our hands dirty. Literally. Enter cleaning gloves. Get the right size. Wash the outside of the gloves when you're done. If you're separating cleaning gloves from dishwashing gloves, get different colors or use a marker to label them.

- **cleaning apron**

Sometimes we don't want to get our clothes dirty either. As an alternative to cleaning naked, use an apron. Not the same one you use for cooking, but rather one you won't mind getting a little grimy.

- **step stool**

  Get one light enough to carry around the house. Make sure it will allow you to get high enough to reach cobwebs and the top of the refrigerator.

- **good broom & dust pan**

  Choose a broom with angled bristled to get into those corners. Dust pans with a rubbery edge helps the pan rest flush against the floor and thus is able to pick up more dirt.

  Hang brooms rather than propping them against a wall. The weight of the broom resting on the bristles causes them to break and get misshapen. When bristles become bent or sparse, get a new broom. It makes a noticeable different to have a new, well functioning broom and dust pan.

  Don't use the same broom inside the house that you use outside. Heavy outside work is tough on brooms and exposes them to dirt you don't want to bring back into the house. Get a heavy duty broom for outdoor cleaning.

- **vacuum cleaner**

  For homes with carpets and heavy rugs. If you've only hard flooring, you can skip the vacuum cleaner altogether but a low-pile vacuum cleaner is still very helpful to get into the cracks of hardwood floors.

  Side tip on vacuuming: Keep furniture at least one vacuum head width apart so you aren't moving furniture every time you vacuum.

- **hand vacuum cleaner**

  This is more like a "nice to have" than a "must have." A hand - vac is very helpful everywhere from the couch cushions to stairs to the car. It's perfect for sucking up cobwebs and relieves the labor of hauling around a full size vacuum cleaner for small jobs.

- **mop/mopping system**

  Choose a floor cleaning method that works well for you. Refer to the upcoming chapter on cleaning floors to help you make a choice of what system is best for you.

- **bucket or dishpan**

  Designate a bucket or tub to be used just for cleaning. Be sure that mop and squeegee heads fit comfortably into the tub. Dishpans work well, as they are shallow and wide - though they do lack a handle.

must have cleaners...

With regular maintenance and light cleaning, harsh chemicals for tough jobs will be largely unnecessary. Cleaners are available at the store or in your own kitchen. Choose what works best for you.

here's what you'll need for most house. It's not a lot.

- **glass cleaner**

  To shine up mirrors, glass and faucets. Use commercial glass cleaner or use full strength vinegar for a streak-free shine.

- **all purpose cleaner**

  There are plenty of all purpose cleaners on the shelves to choose from. To make an all purpose cleaner, dissolve 1/4 cup of borax, 1/4 cup of vinegar in two quarts of hot water. This mixture can be poured into a squirt bottle or used straight from the bucket.

- **bleach**

  Most surfaces should not be cleaned with bleach, even when the bleach is diluted. In fact, bleach doesn't even clean. It is only meant to kill bacteria or whiten. Bleach is helpful mostly for toilets and laundry. It can discolor and degrade the item you mean to clean, so be careful.

- **carpet spot cleaner**

Use carpet cleaners with caution. Commercial carpet spot cleaners can leave behind a residue that actually attracts dirt. We'll go into cleaning both hard floor and carpets in more depth in the floor cleaning section.

- **furniture cleaner & polish**
  Refer to the section on cleaning floors for good options and help making your own.

Store all cleaners and chemicals out of reach of children - even natural ones. Natural doesn't mean safe or innocuous. Cyanide is natural. Keep it all at a comfortable adult level in a clean, dry place. It's difficult enough to get yourself excited about cleaning; it needn't to be made worse by keeping supplies in the dark, cramped conditions under the kitchen sink.

have on hand...
Whether you mix up your own cleaners or not, there are four important agents to have on hand. You'll recognize some from the list of laundry essentials.

- **borax**
  A disinfectant and color-safe alternative to bleach. It comes as a powder which can be diluted with water or mixed into a paste. Keep a jar of it in the bathroom and a box in the laundry room and use it on just about everything that needs disinfecting.

- **white vinegar**
  A rinsing agent and natural disinfectant. It is also good for neutralizing odors. Vinegar is very inexpensive and can be purchased by the gallon. Used in cleaning and in laundry, keep a good amount around. Don't worry, the smell goes away pretty quickly after use.

- **baking soda**
  A gentle abrasive and a natural deodorizer. Typically abrasives are a bad idea as they can scratch the surface. But baking soda

is gentle enough to use on all household surfaces. It's very useful as a paste to work out gunk from around faucets and in corners. Best friend to the toothbrush.

- **club soda**
  This will be used mostly to extract fresh stains from carpets. Flood the fresh spill with club soda and watch it pour out of the fibers. The soda can be 'flat' so don't throw away that half bottle in the back of the refrigerator - put it in the cleaning closet for later.

We can skip some of the work of carrying cleaning supplies around by preparing a cleaning supply caddy to stash on each floor of the house or in each bathroom.

Fill the caddy with only the supplies to be used in that area. No furniture polish. Just a simple collection - such as glass cleaner, all-purpose cleaner and some cleaning cloths. Keep other supplies in a secondary space. Carve out a pleasant place to store these caddies where they won't be in the way in that room.

Cleaning Floors

Hard floors need a daily sweep and a mopping as necessary. For carpeted areas, a quick vacuum now and then does the job.

choosing a mop...
The most common ways to clean the floor are 1) string mops, 2) sponge mops, 3) cloth head mops and 4) disposal mopping systems.

String mops catch a lot of grime and easily cover a large area. But it requires wringing - often by hand, although some have a wringing mechanism. The water is hot and string mop heads are very heavy. Wash the head in hot water when you're through. It has to be dried all the way through, as the thick fibers won't dry in a cupboard, so never put it away damp. String mops are best for mopping up large liquid messes and aren't as useful in a home setting.

Sponge mops have a mechanism in the handle to make hand wringing unnecessary. The damp sponge grows bacteria and needs to be replaced frequently. Replaceable heads are relatively inexpensive, widely available and straightforward to change. The main complaint about sponge mops is that they are essentially unable to pick up any dirt left behind after sweeping. It's very important to sweep well before washing and may be necessary to sweep again after the clean floors dry.

Cloth mops have a plastic or metal frame with a cloth covered head. The cloth is most often a terry cloth or microfiber fabric. The main drawback is that they are extremely difficult to rinse out - requiring that you actually take off the cloth cover every time you rinse it out. Then you rinse, wring it out and put the cloth back on the mop head. That means frequent contact with hot, dirty water. On the plus side, these pads are machine washable.

There are a number of mopping systems featuring **disposable moist cleaning pads**. These are instant gratification tools - minimal prep and quick results. The pads are wet wipes. When you've finished the job, just toss the pad in the trash.

However, as with the sponge mop, this method doesn't allow for picking up or removing dislodged debris well. Next, it's always better to clean renewably. Finally, such systems are too expensive to use on a daily basis.

Mops degrade due to water, cleaner and tough work. Throw away or wash them if there is any sign of mildew or breaking.

For small areas, washing the floor by hand is surprisingly efficient. You use less water and avoid the trouble of getting out a mop and bucket. Use a cloth or sponge to wash the floor. Hand washing is also a great way to spot clean when you're short on time. Dirt attracts dirt, so always wipe up spots as you see them.

how to wash floors...
There are plenty of products on store shelves formulated for hard flooring. However, in most cases, hot water and soap really is the best way to go. Nearly every surface, including porous floors, can stand up to water and soap. That being said, if you're concerned about how it will affect the your floor, test a hidden section before mopping.

Clear out movable furniture so you can mop under it. Sweep or (vacuum) the floor. Hand vacuum cleaners are useful for cleaning in the cracks and hard to sweep places.

After sweeping the floor well, spray all-purpose cleaner on any particularly dirty spots. Let it sit for a minute or two while you prepare your washing water.

Fill a bucket with hot water and your chosen cleaner. Working in small sections, mop the floor. Keep a plastic bristle brush in the pocket of your cleaning apron for easy access. For particularly dirty spots, use the stiff brush to scrub it clean. Rinse and wring out the mop as you move to another small section.

Put some muscle into it. Cleaner and the scrub brush will make the work easier but won't do all the work. Be sure you're not just spreading water around.

After mopping, go over the clean floor again using fresh, hot water to rinse.

Mop your way out of the room, with the wash bucket positioned by the door (the last place you will mop). When you're done mopping, allow the floor to air dry completely before putting back removed furniture.

cleaning specific floorings...

Stone flooring can be washed with plain soap, just as with most floors. Take care not to use to much cleaner or soap. Change your rinse water frequently.

Never use any acids, including vinegar. Abrasives and ammonia-based cleaners should also be kept away from stone. All of these can dull the floor's luster.

Ceramic flooring, both glazed and unglazed can be washed with plain hot water and soap. Glazed tiles clean up nicely, but unglazed ceramic tiles are porous and can stain in the process of everyday life. TSP and other commercial products can draw out some of those stains. The easiest way to handle unglazed tiles is simply to glazed them. If the thought of glazing them breaks your heart, don't do it. Just leave it as is and consider those stains part of the character of the floor.

Do not use strong abrasives, heavy brushes or steel wool on tile. Not only will it scratch the tile, but those scratches will eventually fill with dirt and be horrible to clean next time. Don't use bleach often, as it will eventually discolor the grout. Don't use bleach at all on unglazed tiles. Be very careful with tiles, as too much force can cause them to chip or crack.

With **hardwood floors**, the type of wood is less important than the type of finish. The easiest finish to clean is good old sealant. Stained, unfinished and penetrating seals must first be waxed. Hardwood floors can be mopped with simple soap and water. The key is to mop small areas at a time, drying as you go. Wood expands when it's wet, causing damage and cracking of the floor. Keep liquid exposure to a minimum.

Treat **carpeting** with a protectant that will repel stains. This doesn't mean spills can be left and cleaned up later. Protectant will make is a little easier to clean but will not take the place of cleaning.

Save time and wear and tear on the carpet by only vacuuming high traffic zones, such as the main area of the common living spaces. Corners and edges don't experience as much debris and dirt as well used areas do.

For odor problems, sprinkle the floor with baking soda. Let the baking soda sit for a while and then vacuum it up. There are also commercial powders for this, often with a scent of its own added.

Surface cleaning delays the need for more damaging shampooing of carpets. For spills, reach for the club soda. Flood the spot with club soda. The spot will pour out of the carpet. Using an old towel, blot the area with a thick cloth. Use good pressure, allowing the towel to absorb the liquid making its way into the carpet fibers. Blot, but don't rub. The first time I skeptically tried the club soda treatment, I was hooked. It really works.

Apply commercial carpet spot cleaner according to the directions on the package. Usual procedure is to saturate the area, let it sit for a few minutes and then blot up the cleaner as you did with the original spill.

For stairs, vacuum (with a stand up or hand held) the main area. Wipe the corners of each stair with a damp rag if your vacuum cleaner can't get to them. The rag will snatch up animal hair and crumbs in the those hard to reach places.

Cleaning & Polishing Furniture

"Vinegar and oil, rubbed in with flannel, and the furniture rubbed with a clean duster, produce a very good polish."

- Book of Household Management #2309

Basic furniture cleaner for finished wood is:

1 part acid to 1 part oil.

The acid cleans the wood, while the oil treats it. That's pretty much it. Adjust the ratio of acid to oil according to your preferences.

common acids: Lemon juice, white vinegar, apple cider vinegar
common oils: Mineral oil, olive oil, vegetable oil

Vegetable oil and white vinegar makes a very good polish and these ingredients are usually on hand. Mix together the acid and oil. While you *can* store the mixture in a spray bottle, it's best to make a fresh batch for each cleaning. Add a few drops of essential oil - lemon, lavender, rose, etc.- for a nice scent.

let's get started...
Clean the wood with simple soap and water. We don't want to polish over dust and residue. Wash the gunk off well. Wipe dry with a clean cloth right away.

For dull finishes, give wood the *tea treatment*. The tea removes the build up that blocks oil from penetrating into the wood. Steep two bags of regular tea in a cup of boiling water. Cool the tea to room temperature. Again, working in small sections, wash the wood with the cooled tea. Depending on the state of the wood, this simple step - removing old build up - is sufficient to bring out a nice shine.

Now on to *polishing*. Dip a clean, dry cloth into the acid/oil mixture and wipe into the wood. Work in small sections, wiping the furniture with a second dry cloth. Buff. The best cloths for furniture cleaning are 100% cotton flannel, old cloth diapers and microfiber.

Equal parts interest and history, below is another of Mrs. Beeton's own furniture polish recipes.

"Ingredients - Equal proportions of linseed-oil, turpentine, vinegar and spirits of wine. Mode - When used, shake the mixture well, and rub on the furniture with a piece of linen rag, and polish with a clean duster."

- Book of Household Management #2309

Speaking of history, *never* clean antiques. The surest way to destroy the value of a piece is to clean it. Just dust the piece and appreciate its vintage unless recommended otherwise by a professional antiques appraiser.

Doing Laundry

"The laundry-maid is charged with the duty of washing and getting up the family linen - a situation of great importance where the washing is all done at home."

- Book of Household Management #2372

The laundry space is already prepared for success. It's stocked with everything you need. Ready to go.

let's get started...

sorting laundry

Before washing, there is sorting. Clothes can either be separated when they come into laundry room or be sorted as they go into the washing machine.

The downside of sorting from a large pile of dirty laundry directly into the washing machine is that dirty, wet laundry doesn't get more fun to sort as it lays in a pile of other dirty, wet laundry. Try to sort laundry as soon as you get your hands on it. Only resort to a single dirty clothes basket if there's a space crunch.

If you can, use 3 baskets: one for delicate wash, one for hot water loads and one for general laundry. The general guideline for washing laundry is that cotton should be washed on high, while synthetics on medium or low. But read clothing labels and wash the piece accordingly.

"Every article having been examined and assorted, the sheets and fine linen should be placed in one of the tubs and just covered with lukewarm water, in which a little soda has been dissolved and mixed, and left there to soak until the morning."

- Book of Household Management #2374

As you toss clothes into the washer, check pockets, zip zippers, hook bra hooks and see that buttons are firmly attached. Remove sashes and belts and clean them separately. If you can get the rest of the household to do this before they toss their clothes in the laundry basket, all the better.

washing laundry
Modern washing machines do all of the work of dispensing soap, fabric softener and bleach. Add each to the appropriate slots, rinse the slot with a little water and press start. Done.

Resist the temptation to use more detergent than the bottle recommends. Excessive soap leaves residue that attracts dirt, making clothing look dingy.

If your washing machine doesn't have a built in dispenser for soap and such, it's a little more work. Add bleach and detergent to the water before adding clothes. Add fabric softener during the final rinse cycle. If you're using fabric softener sheets, toss one in to the dryer along with wet clothing. The softener will dispense into the clean clothes during the drying process.

washing specific fabrics

delicates: lace, hosiery, lingerie, etc.

Delicate trumps color or temperature. White lace goes with delicates, not with bleach loads, for example. Each piece will have its own washing requirements. Most delicate fabrics require hand washing, though many can be machine washed with cold water and gentle cleanser.

Don't bleach delicates. Bleach is hard on fibers and delicate fabrics will not survive long.

Hang dry or air tumble in the dryer. Any pieces that could suffer from stretching must be laid flat on a towel, not line dried. Lay the wet piece on a dry towel and shape it as you would like it to dry.

Delicate items should also not be 'wrung out.' Lay the clean and still wet delicate piece on a towel. Roll up the towel with the delicate inside of it. This gently presses out all of the water without stressing the fibers. This is especially helpful with hosiery and lace. Unroll the towel and allow the damp piece to air dry the rest of the way.

delicates: swim wear

Soak swimwear in cold water after swimming to rinse out salt and/or chlorine as soon as it's taken off. After a big family swim, just fill the bathtub and tell everyone to throw their swimsuits into it.

Wash the swimwear in cold water without bleach and with minimal soap. This is easier to do by hand in the sink than using the washing machine.

delicates: wool

Wash wool in cold water, preferable by hand. Never use hot water or dry wool with heat or by hanging on a line. Heat will shrink the wool and line drying will stretch it out. Instead, dry

flat on a towel, shaping the garment first. Shape clothing by
laying it flat and literally shaping it to your body.

general laundry: darks & lights
For small families and those who don't let laundry build up long,
it's alright to wash darks and lights in the same load. Unless there
is a reason to believe otherwise, it's safe to assume all the colors
will survive the wash together. Throw a lavender shirt in with a
brown sock and likely no tragedy will befall you. The puritanical
fascination with separating lights and darks is truly unnecessary
unless it's the first time you've washed the piece.

For those with the mania and time to do this serious sorting,
general laundry can be sorted into light colors (pastels), darks
(black, navy, green, etc.) and wilds (red, orange, and such).

general wash: bleaching whites
Wash whites in warm water with bleach. All whites can be dried
together on medium or hight heat. Remove synthetics from the
dryer as soon as they are dry and leave cottons in as they take
longer to dry.

general wash: tough fabrics
Jeans and other rough fabrics get a load to themselves. Their
heavy zippers and coarse material can be hard on other clothing
sharing the wash or dryer.

Only turn denim inside out when attempting to protect
against fading. For very dirty denim leave them the right way out
to assure all that debris makes its way out of the folds.

hot wash: towels
Towels, both those from the kitchen and those from the bathroom,
should be washed in hot water. Because towels absorb water, they
often hold onto water, breeding bacteria as they dry slowly on the

towel bar. Hot water and high heat drying will take care of this. Be sure towels are completely dry before being folded and put in the closet.

hot wash: sheets

Wash sheets in their own load, by bed. This way everything comes out of the dryer at the same time and the bed can be made without waiting on a missing pillowcase.

Wash sheets in hot water, adding bleach for white sheets. Prevent wrinkles by taking sheets out of the dryer as soon as they're dry.

hot wash: cloth diapers

Diapers have a laundry system all their own. First, procure a medium size bucket with a lid that seals. Fill the bucket 3/4 full with cold water. (Make sure you can still lift the bucket at that point, because it's going to get a whole lot heavier when it's full of diapers as well.) The lid is to contain spills but also for safety. Add vinegar and borax. There is no need for bleach or soap in this water. This is the diaper hamper - where wet and (empty and rinsed out) dirty diapers and covers are placed to soak while they wait to be washed.

Plan to wash diapers every other day. Stock enough cloth diapers and covers to last two or three full days, but don't go too long between washings.

When it comes time to wash the diapers, drain out as much water from the bucket as possible. Pouring the excess liquid into the toilet works best.

Wash diapers hot with soap and without bleach or fabric softener. Add vinegar during the load's final rinse to strip away the last of the soap. Baby bottoms are sensitive and soap residue is not good for them. Dry hot until they are bone dry. They can be line dried; but still make sure they are absolutely dry before they go back to the nursery.

dry clean only fabrics
Dry cleaning is a lovely example of factoring in cost of care when making a purchase. By cautious as to how many 'dry clean only' items there are in the family's combined wardrobe. It's expensive to have them professionally cleaned and not a very 'green' way to launder clothing. The chemicals used in dry cleaning (specifically perchloroethylene, also called 'perc') cause damage to the liver, kidneys and nervous systems. These are not pretty afflictions. We bring these toxins into our homes right along with the plastic garment covers and paper covered hangers. These chemicals are obviously not something to which we want to expose our neighbors, children and environment.

ironing

> *"Ironing is a part of the duties of a lady's-maid, and she should be able to do it in the most perfect manner when it becomes necessary."*
>
> - Book of Household Management #2282

As with doing the wash, turn to the labels when ironing and set the iron temperature accordingly. If no instructions are listed, generally, cotton needs high heat, while synthetics require a cooler iron.

Don't iron directly on embellishments. Rather iron on the reverse side or cover the design with a cloth before ironing. For lightweight or delicate pieces, put the press cloth over the piece and iron through the cloth. The opposite applies to cotton and rayon, which tend to get more wrinkles. Iron those directly on the right side. Iron collars and cuffs on both sides, as they are thick and need to be wrinkle free on both sides.

Don't iron over buttons, zippers, or other fasteners. It's not good for the fasteners or the iron.

Ease out wrinkles with a spray of water directly to the fabric before ironing. Even with an iron with steam, it's often easier to squirt the piece with a spray bottle than to drain the iron. The iron's water reservoir never seems to empty completely and then drips all over the laundry room when you put it away.

Lots of ironing in your household? Invest in a clothes press. The press applies both heat and pressure for a crisp finished piece. You still have to monitor and operate the press, but it's strength saving and does a quality job.

ironing sheets
Avoid wrinkly sheets by taking them from the dryer before they are completely dry. Put the bottom sheet on the bed. It will quickly dry taut on the bed and wrinkle-free. Iron the pillowcases. As the bed linens are still damp (from being pulled from the dryer early, the wrinkles will melt out as you iron.

Top sheets are flat, making for no hard-to-iron angles. But they are also large and cumbersome. Only put real effort into ironing the top part of the sheet that will fold over and show on the bed.

Not into ironing sheets? Get something in a wrinkle-free fabric.

Seasonal Deep Cleaning

*"Besides the daily routine which we have described,
there are portions of every house which can only be
thoroughly cleaned occasionally; at which time the
whole house usually undergoes a more thorough
cleaning than is permitted in the general way."*
- Book of Household Management #2326

A home gets pretty dirty in 6 months, even with a focused housekeeper. Good news is this makes seasonal cleaning immensely rewarding. The hard work is worth doing when it makes such a difference. And after all, it only comes twice a year. Schedule your cleanings most logically for your family and climate. Spring is really anytime after the thaw when it's warm enough outside to open windows and air out the house. Fall is when activities out doors start to cool and inside the house becomes the main social hub.

The two seasonal cleanings don't need to be precisely six months apart. There is a much greater chance of success if you do it on your own time schedule. It just needs to be done. Take a week, take a few weeks to get the job done throughly. I sometimes do kitchen deep cleaning a week before the cleaning for the rest of the house so that I can take a nice break between the two big jobs.

> *"The spring is the usual period set apart for house-cleaning, and removing all the dust and dirt which will necessarily, with the best of housewives, accumulate during the winter months."*
> - Book of Household Management #61

Spring is a time of opening up. The air rushing in open windows seems Nature's way of telling us to liven up and shake off the dust. The first good day in the spring, open up the house and roll up your sleeves.

> *"As winter approaches, this house-cleaning will have to be repeated, and the warm bed and window curtains replaced."*
> - Book of Household Management #2328

Fall cleaning and maintenance is best done in the weeks before chilly weather sets in and the house will have to be shut up to keep warm. Fortunately, blustery days inspire burrowing and nesting. Use that internal jolt to clean the house and bed it for the winter.

Each room needs the same treatment - a thorough cleaning. Everything should look pretty nice and shiny when we're done.

Scrubbing baseboards and table legs may not seem like it would make a difference, but it leaves a fresh feeling and is worth the work.

Lay in a good supply rags and paper towels before taking on seasonal cleaning. Inventory cleaning supplies and tools, too. Elbow deep in housework is not the time to run to the store to restock.

let's get started...

After getting the room to its general state of tidiness, start with deep cleaning. A list of seasonal cleaning jobs is in the 'resources' section at the end of this book. Check off each job as you do it.

in each room:

- sanitize everything. Daily it is best to use the most mild cleaners you can but during seasonal cleaning bust out the disinfectant.
- dust everything! As always, top down. We keep on top of surface dusting, but there are places we can't reach on a daily basis. Get up on the stool and track down those places.
- wash window tracks
- clean doorknobs and light switch plates. Everyone uses these all the time. Get the germs off. In fact, cleaning knobs and switch plates is a good idea after every round of sickness in the house.
- wash windows on both sides. Inside, spray the glass and wipe it down. Outside window washing can be almost fun. There is no fear of splashing water on the ground because you're outside. Scrub the window with a regular sponge and regular soap. Glass cleaner isn't necessary on exterior windows. Rinse the window. For large exterior windows, you can even just use the hose to rinse it down. Squeegee the glass top to bottom. Between each stroke, wipe off the rubber.

- wash window treatments as necessary. If they aren't dirty, skip it. Do dust blinds.
- scrub baseboards
- scrub both sides of interior doors and door jambs
- polish furniture. Brush up on how to do this in the chapter "Cleaning & Polishing Furniture"
- clean out closets and cupboards of unused items. Check expiration dates. Make a list of items to replace. For instance, more cornstarch or a new wire whisk.
- line drawers, shelves and cupboards with fresh liners or wash the liners you're already using. Replace illegible labels.
- clean behind and under furniture. We do this on a regular basis, but we don't often move the heavy stuff such as sofas and sideboards.
- spot wash walls, high and low. Touch up paint.
- scrub floors
- polish/shine hardwood floors
- vacuum carpets & rugs
- return borrowed items inevitably found in the course of deep cleaning

floors

Floors get mopped and vacuumed regularly. Now focus on those cracks and corners. Pull out and clean behind furniture. Take the time to actually move what you can and vacuum or sweep. Once again, it's only twice a year and cuts down on dust bunnies and allergens. It's best if it can be moved to another room while you attend to the floors. Take out rugs and floor lamps as well. Sweep or vacuum behind *everything*. For hard floors, mop like you've never mopped before. This is the best mop these floors are getting for six months. This means using a toothbrush in the corners and around door jams.

Shampooing carpets is a hassle and is tough on fibers so do it as infrequently as you can get away with. Carpet cleaning is not a costly job to hire out, which is probably the best thing to do with little ones underfoot. Shampooers are also available for rent at most large grocery stores.

Find out how long it will take for the carpets to dry. Have a plan for how to pass that time. Go to the park and resist temptation to come home early. Carpets are most vulnerable to stains and attracting dirt while they are drying after a cleaning. When it's all dry, vacuum the carpets again to fluff them back up.

If the carpets are in good condition - needing no cleaning - yay! Skip shampooing. It's not a preventative measure.

the bathroom

The bathroom ranks amongst the most time-consuming rooms to spring and fall clean. It's time again for the toothbrush treatment. Plan to scrub and disinfect every surface. Use hot water and borax. Be sure to get behind the toilet and in the corners of the floor, areas often missed in routine cleaning.

Soap scum is tough to remove, though regular cleanings have helped to keep the problem in check. Clean it off by using baking soda as a mild abrasive.

- start with thorough regular bathroom cleaning. Complete the daily prompt and do it well. Scrub the shower, shine the cupboards. Do it all.
- bleach any sign of mildew. Bleach is not a cleaning agent, so wash everything well first. Cleaners specifically to cut through soap residue are also available and is very helpful for big jobs.
- use a pumice stone to clean stained toilets. Pumice is softer than is the toilet, allowing the stone to scratch off stains without scratching the bowl. Using a weak bleach solution, clean the toilet inside and outside. Get up *under* the rim. Then wash your eyes out with soap.

- gather everyone's hairbrushes and combs. Remove hair from the bristles. Soak brushes and combs in hot water and vinegar to strip away oily residue left by hair.
- sort through bathing and beauty supplies and toss anything expired.
- evaluate the caulk and replace as necessary. It's inexpensive and minimally difficult to do.

the living room
Seasonal cleaning in the living room is done with just a good job at the daily prompt and the 'in every room' list. For fireplaces, clean the ashes and wash the glass.

the kitchen
Kitchens are a hub for grease and steam, making it a tough cleaning job. Scrub down everything.
- begin with the ceilings and high cabinets and work your way down. When you get to the floor, wash the underside of cabinets and baseboards.
- pull everything out from under the sink. Food meant for the trashcan, forgotten chemicals and newly discovered drips can all be found down here. Give this under sink space a fresh coat of mildew resistant paint if necessary.
- weed through both the refrigerator and the freezer. Remove everything and assess it. Toss expired or unwanted food, condiments, spices and appliances. Wipe out the fridge and freezer of spills and crumbs. Return the food to your shiny new fridge. Wash the exterior of the fridge. Don't forget the top.
- scrub out the oven. Once clean, line the oven to make future messes easier to clean up. Baking sheet liners can be washed but lining the oven with aluminum foil works as well. It's much easier to do that than to scrub the oven.

the bedrooms

After regular deep cleaning, the only thing left to do is flip the mattress. Rotate it end to end as well. Switch linens & blankets for the upcoming season

the children's bedrooms

- wash children's toys, including doll clothes.
- sort toys and keep the ones they are using available. Other toys can be organized and packed up so that later you bring them out and the children feel they got new toys.
- pull beds and cribs away from the wall and get behind them. It's unbelievable what gets stuck back there.

wardrobes

Children grow so quickly that their wardrobes absolutely need a good sort at least twice a year. Such sorts are best done with weather changes. For school-attending children, correspond the fall sort with the start of school. This gives you the best idea of what the children will need for the upcoming school year.

If you buy clothing when it's on sale at the end of the season and save it for the next year, store those clothes with hand-me-downs so as to pull them all out together.

Pack away out grown clothes for the next child or donate them.

For adult wardrobes, launder and store out of season clothes, culling as you go. Pull out last year's clothes. Wash them and fill your drawers with the new season's wardrobe.

Store out of season clothes in a place separate from clothes for this season.

laundry room

Quick work in the laundry room:

- cull laundry supplies. Cut supplies down to just what you need and are using.
- wash laundry baskets
- clean washer inside & out
- clean dryer inside & out

And you're done for another 6 months.

Hiring Help

While working as a maid, I saw homes so untidy I wondered why they'd even bothered to have help come in. We couldn't get to anything. It's impossible to wash countertops buried under stacks of paper.

I worked for one family in which the father wrote sweet notes on the bathroom mirrors when he went out of town. A lovely gesture, but I couldn't clean the bathroom properly without wiping away those notes. The family gave no indication of whether the notes were to stay or go. If you're fortunate enough to have hired help, make the most of it by being ready.

Prepare for domestics (hey, I had to sneak that term *somewhere* after reading Mrs. Beeton) by giving them clear access to the areas and tools they will need. This means picking up clutter lying around. A maid can be expected to do deep and surface cleaning, but s/he will have no idea of where most of your things belong.

Let the family know when the maid will be there so everyone has time to tidy up their things and put away private items.

Make a list of what must be done. Walk through the house as if you had a magic wand. Any disaster you would poof! into cleanliness goes on the list. You can also just give the maid your daily prompt. Mark jobs that are especially important to you and tell your maid to do these tasks first in a time crunch. What is especially important to be done may change from time to time.

This time it might be floors; next time folding laundry might be most important to you. The clients who gave me clear instructions got a house perfectly cleaned to their specifications.

the night before the maid comes...
- tidy every room. Take extra time to make sure everything is accessible.
- print out the list of tasks you'd like completed
- mark the jobs on the list that are especially important to clean this time
- set out cleaners and tools the maid will need

The big question I get about hiring help: do I stay in the house or clear out and let the housekeeper work alone? Either. Stash small children somewhere else. Otherwise, it's whatever you prefer. A quality maid will feel fine with you in the house or not.

Resources

Daily Housekeeping Prompt

❖ ❖ ❖

entry
- tidy
- dust
- cull items on the coat rack
- clean windows & glass
- sweep / vacuum / mop floors

living room
- tidy
- dust
- wipe down surfaces
- clean windows & glass
- vacuum couch & between cushions
- empty trash can
- sweep / vacuum / mop floor

bathrooms
- tidy
- dust
- wipe down mirrors, faucets, countertops & sinks
- wipe rim & inside of the tub
- scrub toilet bowl
- wipe outside of toilet
- scrub shower & tub
- empty trash can
- replenish bathroom supplies (toilet paper, fresh towels)
- sweep / vacuum / mop floor

kitchen

- unload & load dishwasher
- hand wash dishes
- wipe down inside & outside of microwave
- wipe down inside & outside of oven
- wipe down counter appliances
- wash countertops & other surfaces
- wipe down cabinet doors
- wipe windowsills, ledges & shelves
- clean out refrigerator
- wipe inside & outside of fridge
- take out trash & recycling
- sweep floors
- mop floors

dining room

- tidy
- dust
- wipe down table
- wipe down chairs
- wipe down other surfaces
- clean windows & glass
- sweep / vacuum / mop floors

bedrooms

- tidy
- make bed
- dust
- change linens
- wipe down surfaces
- clean windows & glass
- sweep / vacuum / mop floors

Seasonal Cleaning Checklist

❖ ❖ ❖

in every room...
- dust entire room, top down
- clean cobwebs from windows, corners & light fixtures
- wash window tracks
- clean doorknobs & light switch plates
- clean windows inside & out
- launder window treatments
- scrub baseboards
- scrub both sides of interior doors and door jambs
- wash light fixtures inside and out
- polish furniture
- clean out closets & cupboards
- for each drawer, shelf & cupboard:
    - wipe clean
    - replace liners & labels as necessary
- vacuum behind & under furniture
- spot wash walls
- touch up paint
- clean floors
    - scrub floors
    - vacuum carpets & rugs
    - shampoo carpets & wash rugs
    -

bathrooms
- scrub toilet throughly, inside & outside
- clean combs and brushes
- evaluate and replace caulk

living room
- vacuum & spot clean couch
- clean ashes from fireplace
- wash fireplace glass

kitchen
- scrub counters, sinks and faucets
- wash walls with degreaser
- clean microwave inside & out
- clean out refrigerator
- clean refrigerator inside & out
- clean out freezer of old food
- clean oven inside & out
- vacuum refrigerator grill & coils
- clean range / cook top
- wipe down appliances, canisters, etc.
- clean out & scrub area under the sink
- wash out trash can

bedrooms
- flip mattress
- switch linens & blankets for the upcoming season

laundry room
- cull laundry supplies and restock
- wash laundry baskets
- wipe down shelves & surfaces
- clean washer inside & out
- clean dryer inside & out

medicine cabinet
- restock the medicine cabinet, checking for expired medications

wardrobe

for children

- cull clothing and shoes. Evaluate each piece for correct size, season & condition
- sort clothes that will be passed on to the next child into a bag and label with contents (Summer Clothes - Girl - 18-24 months). Store with other clothing awaiting a new owner.
- pull out clothing stored for the new season. Check waiting hand-me-downs for wardrobe additions
- clean clothing pulled out from storage

for adults

- cull through clothing and shoes. Evaluate each piece for correct size, season and condition.
- pull out clothing stored for the new season
- clean clothing pulled from storage

Spring Groundskeeping Checklist

❖ ❖ ❖

- clean out gutters
- wash decks & porches especially if any byproducts of the past season is making the porch slick or dangerous. Common culprits are dirt, moss, sand, & oil.
- remove nests and webs from walls, eaves and corners
- put screens back on windows
- wash exterior doors
- touch-up exterior paint once weather is dry enough for the paint to dry. Remember that paint is a protectant, so keep the exterior in good paint repair.
- clean grill inside & out in preparation for summer
- rake the yard of random debris. There won't be much but check the bushes and other hidden places.
- attend to the air conditioning and other cooling systems in the home. Make sure everything is in working order. If there is a problem, get it fixed.
- bring out exterior furniture and textiles. Many items in general will have been stored away for the wet and cold seasons.

Fall Groundskeeping Checklist

❖ ❖ ❖

- wash & store away window screens
- wash & store away exterior furniture and textiles
- store summer toys. Discard anything that didn't quite make it through the summer, such as broken squirt guns, tangled volleyball net, etc.
- re-home plants too sensitive for upcoming weather
- drain, wash and store garden hoses
- wash exterior doors It's going to be a while before you feel like busting out a bucket of water outside.
- clean grill inside & out. Store the grill if it won't be used in the winter. Either way, have a place for it undercover.
- acquire & stack firewood in cold climates
- check that the furnace is working properly
- buy a winter's supply of furnace filters
- have the chimney inspected and/or cleaned. A cleaning is typically needed for every cord of wood burned or every few years.
- check weather stripping on doors and windows, replacing as necessary
- clean exterior mats of summer dirt and sand and check that they are in good condition for the coming muddy weather. Replace as necessary.
- stock up on salt
- insulate exposed plumbing
- stock up on essentials should the power go out or snowdrifts preventing leaving the house

www.ingramcontent.com/pod-product-compliance
Lightning Source LLC
Chambersburg PA
CBHW070638030426
42337CB00020B/4063